JOURNAL

OF

JAMES HALE,

LATE

SERGEANT

IN THE NINTH REGIMENT OF FOOT.

1826.

The Naval & Military Press Ltd

Published jointly by

The Naval & Military Press Ltd

In reprinting in facsimile from the original, any imperfections are inevitably reproduced and the quality may fall short of modern type and cartographic standards.

ADVERTISEMENT.

IT is presumed that these pages will be found not altogether uninteresting to the general reader, though it is right to state that they are printed chiefly with a view to the benefit of the poor man, the writer of them. The Journal was originally compiled for his own satisfaction, and without any intention whatever of making it public. During a protracted state of bodily suffering, attended with some peculiar circumstances of domestic distress, he has found an amusement in revising what he had written; and now he has been advised to get it printed, in the hope of adding somewhat to the narrow allowance on which he has to support himself and his motherless children.

The principal errors in the grammar and spelling have been corrected; and a very few sentences have been omitted: otherwise the Journal appears as in his own hand-writing.

OCT. 31, 1826.

JOURNAL.

ON the 4th of April, 1808, I enlisted to serve his Majesty, King GEORGE the Third, in the Royal North Gloucester Regiment of Militia, commanded by Colonel Kingscote, for the small bounty of five guineas; and Cirencester being head quarters of the North Gloucester, I joined the regiment at that place, and there we remained till towards the latter end of May; when, rather to our surprise, we received orders from government to march to Portsmouth, a large seaport town in Hampshire. By this time, we had nearly learned our duty; but not one-third of the regiment had got their clothing: but we each had a soldier's cap, and a tail about eighteen inches long, placed on our heads; and in this miserable looking figure we marched through the country, from Cirencester to Portsmouth.

On the 19th of May, we commenced our route, and marched to Swindon; the 20th, to Marlborough; the 21st, to Collingbourn; the 22d, we halted; the 23d, we marched to Andover; the 24th, to Winchester; the 25th, to Wickham; and the 26th, to Portsmouth; and took up our quarters in Portsea Barracks. At this place our duty was very hard; for I may venture to say, that we were every other night on duty, nearly the whole of the time we were there. The garrison was commanded by ——— Whitelock, who was a noble fellow to keep us out of idleness. However, I did not stop at Portsmouth long; for in September, orders were given for four companies of our regiment to march to Cumberland Fort, (a place about seven miles from Portsmouth,) in order to assist in doing some king's works that were to be done in that fort; and also, to do duty over some convicts that were on board the hulks near that place. The barracks in that fort were all under ground. There we remained till March, 1804; when we received the route to march to Silver-hill barracks, in Sussex; and on the 10th we marched to Chichester; the 11th, we halted, being Sunday, and attended divine service; the 12th, to Arundel, the 13th, to Shoreham; the 14th, to Lewes; and the 15th, to Silver-hill barracks.

This was a very pleasant place in the summer, having a most beautiful prospect of the fields and groves for a great distance all around, but no town nor village within our bounds. This was very teazing to us; as no soldier dare be seen more than one mile from his quarters, except with a written pass from his commanding officer, or he would be deemed a deserter. But to the great misfortune of our regiment, there was one thing rather more alarming than that; that was, as we supposed, bad water: for in a few days after our arrival at that place, our men began to fall down with sickness, more or less every day, for some time; and in three or four weeks, our hospital was crowded with sick, and many poor soldiers were summoned to their last home in a very short time: the well was of a considerable depth, and the water tasted very very disagreeable. Fortunately, we did not remain there long: for on the 5th of September, we marched to Cliffend camp, near Pett, about   miles from Hastings, on the sea coast, (together with a party of engineers), for the purpose of doing king's works. Our camp was formed within one hundred yards of the sea; and in two or three days after our arrival there, when such arrangements had been made as were necessary, we were all hands put to work, making batteries and breast-works, except a few that were left to do the camp duty: for as there were no fortifications along that part of the coast, nor any troops stationed there, a party of French would frequently land in the night, and take away some of the cattle off the marsh; or otherwise, the smugglers did take them, for it was a noted place for smuggling. We remained there and continued our work as long as the weather would permit us to lay in our tents; then we received orders to march to Stening barracks, in Sussex, for winter quarters; and on the 1st of November we marched to Battle; the 2d, to Lewes; and the 3d, to Stening barracks. This was but a small town, but clean in general, and the inhabitants were very friendly; our barracks were very good, and situated on a pleasant spot of ground close to the town. We remained there as comfortable as soldiers could wish, having nothing but our own regimental duty to do, till the latter end of May, 1805, at which time we received the route from government to march to Bristol. On the 31st of May, we marched to Petworth; June 1st, to Petersfield; the 2d, we halted, being Sunday, and attended divine service; the 3d, to Botley; the 4th, to Rumsey; the 5th, to Salisbury; the 6th, to Devizes; the 7th, to Bath; and the 8th, to Bristol.

Being now returned to our own county, the inhabitants received us with smiles; the streets were crowded with our relations and countrymen, who came to welcome us into the city, and the landlords treated us in every respect with friendship. At this place we had plenty of duty, but not very hard, although it lay very wide; having to do duty over the French prisoners at Stapleton, which was about five miles from College Green, at which place we always assembled, when for duty, let the weather be rough or smooth, by which we frequently got very wet before we could reach our respective guards; and should we be ever so wet, we were never permitted even to take off our accoutrements to dry ourselves a little. However, having good quarters and kind treatment, we did not mind such difficulties as those; for the inhabitants continued very agreeable and friendly during the whole time that we remained there, which was till the 1st of April, 1807, when we received orders from government to leave our own county once more, and proceed to Plymouth.

On the 1st of April, we commenced our route, and marched to Wells; the 2d, to Somerton; the 3d, we halted; the 4th, to Taunton; the 5th, we halted, being Sunday, and attended divine service; the 6th, to Tiverton; the 7th, to Crediton; the 8th, to Oakhampton; the 9th, we halted; the 10th, to Tavistock; and the 11th, to Plymouth, and took up our quarters in Stonehouse barracks; at this place we had a very pleasant prospect, being on a hill close to the mouth of the harbour, having a view of all the shipping that passed in or out; and also, the view of Lord Edgecombe's park and great house, which was on the opposite side of the harbour, just in front of our barracks. The barracks were very good, and made on a very convenient plan; but being situated so high and so near the sea, they were very much exposed to wind and weather, and the duty was rather hard. However, I did not remain there long; for as there was no hopes of a peace, I was rather inclined to extend my service, so that I might have the opportunity of seing some other country; for I was then got quite tired of rambling about England, although the militia service is nothing but a mere pleasure, in general: therefore, as there was an order from government for a general volunteering from the militia, to fill up the regiments of the line, I volunteered my service on the 23d of August, 1807, to serve seven years in his Majesty's 9th or Britannia regiment of foot,

for the bounty of ten guineas, provided his Majesty
should for so long require my service; and also, for
such further period as should be required, but not to
exceed three years in any case whatever. One hundred
and seventy volunteered from the North Gloucester in
about three or four hours, every man for the 9th, that
serviceable old regiment, that had so many times distinguished themselves in their king and country's cause,
when in front of their enemy: and I am happy to.say,
that their character was never stained during the late
war in the Peninsula.

To prevent all irregularity that might have taken
place in the garrison, during the volunteering, it was
thought most proper to send such men as had volunteered to some place by themselves, till they had spent
their money: therefore, on the following day, we were
all marched off to Tavistock, a town about 14 miles
from Plymouth, that being the place appointed for all
the volunteers to assemble at, that belonged to that
district. As soon as we arrived there, and took up our
quarters, we received five guineas each man, in part of
our bounty; and the other five were to be paid when
we joined our regiment. Tavistock is not so large as
Cirencester; and I consider there were more than
two thousand soldiers quartered there, that had volunteered from the different regiments in that district: and
the town being so crowded with drunken men, you may
easily suppose what confusion there was among us, for
drinking and gaming was all that was thought about
as long as the money lasted. However, it did not hold

long: for in about five or six days, many had not the
price of one pint of beer. We remained in that town
fourteen days, by which time the money was nearly all
gone, and most of the men were got quite sober; when
orders were given for the whole to proceed to their
different stations; and as the 9th regiment lay in Ireland at that time, all that belonged to that regiment
were marched back to Plymouth, in order to be in
readiness to embark for Ireland as soon as a ship could
be got ready.

On the 14th of September, 1807, we embarked;
but in consequence of contrary winds, we were obliged
to remain in Plymouth Sound until the 18th, in the
morning, when the wind changed rather in our favour;
and it being a fine clear morning, with a steady breeze,
signal was made to weigh our anchor and put to sea
with all speed, and to steer our course for the Cove of
Cork, in Ireland. Having put to sea, all speed was
made that was possible; the weather continued very
pleasant until the 22d following, by which time we
were got into the Irish Sea; but towards the evening of
that day, a heavy gale of wind sprung up, quite contrary for us, and the sea run very rough, and we could
see by the motions of the captain of the ship, that we
were in great danger; for all the soilders were ordered
to keep below, that we might not interrupt the sailors,
and two or three attempts were made to nail down the
hatchways, for fear the ship would be swamped. As most
of us were young soldiers, and this our first voyage at
sea, you may easily suppose what sort of a stew we were

8

in; one sick here, and another there; and I might say, nearly all were sea-sick. In this miserable condition we beat up and down for two days and nights; till at length, as the captain of the ship could see no hopes of any alteration in the weather, he thought most proper to put into Waterford, if there were a possibility, which place happened to be within a few hours' sail; therefore we put into that harbour, and threw out two anchors, by which we weathered the remainder of the time that we were on board middling well.

We remained in that harbour three days, waiting for fair weather: but as the wind still continued blowing in our teeth, we received orders from the General, that commanded at Waterford, to disembark. We were immediately put on shore at Passage, a village about seven miles from the city of Waterford, and as soon as we had got a little refreshment, we marched to Waterford the same day. The streets in that town were very dirty, and such houses as I went into were not much better. I and one more were quartered on a poor labouring man, (for there are not the same regulations in that country as in England, for there, all the inhabitants, both rich and poor, take their share of soldiers when on the march, more or less according to their abilities), and after some difficulty, I found my quarters. The house appeared, outside, as if it was not a very poor family that belonged to it: but when I entered, not being acquainted with the manner of the country, I began to make some excuse, and asked the people if they would be pleased to direct me to such a place?

9

at the same time showing my billet: upon which, the
poor man desired me and my comrade to sit down;
but I still refused, not thinking that was my quarters,
until the man assured me, that was the place. The
man and his family were sat nose and knees together,
over a bit of fire that was made on the hearth-stone;
and in one corner of the house was a large pig a-grunt-
ing: a hurdle was placed across the angle, which formed
a sort of sty. In a few minutes after I delivered my
billet, I saw the woman very busily employed, scrub-
bing some potatoes with a birch broom, but she was not
very particular, for in about five minutes, the potatoes
were in a large iron pot, and placed over the fire; by
which I concluded they were for the pig: but as soon as
they were done, and the water poured from them, I
saw a hoop placed on the table, and the potatoes turned
out of the pot on the table, without any plate or dish; for
this hoop was meant to keep the potatoes from rolling off
the table. This being done, the family placed themselves
round the table, each with a small cup of milk;
a sea was a.so put for me and my comrade, and the
man desired us to come to the table and take our suppers; but we refused, telling him that we,had supped;
for I could neither see knife, fork, bread, nor meat:
but it was astonishing to see how active they were in
taking the rind off the potatoes with their finger nails.
The whole time they were at supper, the pig continued
grunting and grumbling, but they did not seem to take
any notice of that till they had done, and then what was
left was given to the pig. When supper was cleared

away, we asked them to show us our bed; upon which we were immediately led into another apartment, and in one corner was a heap of straw, but neither sheet, nor blanket, nor any thing else.

On the following day, we marched to Carrick-on-Suire. I have nothing to say in behalf of that town, in regard to cleanliness, either in the streets or houses; my accommodation was much the same as at Waterford, only that I was not accompanied with a pig. I was quartered on a poor man that was one hundred and eight years of age; he had three generations living with him: I mean his own children, his children's children, and their children, all under the same roof. This poor old man could go to a spring that was about two or three hundred yards from his house, and fetch a pitcher of water, with only the small assistance of a walking-stick.

Next day, we marched to Clonmell, in the county of Tipperary. This was a large town, and middling clean; and the inhabitants appeared much cleaner than in many other places, and my accommodation was better than it had been, although I was quartered on a poor labouring man, as before. Next day, we marched to Clogheen; there our treatment was but middling. Next day, we marched to Fermoy, in the county of Cork, which place was the head quarters for the 9th regiment at that time. When we got within about three or four miles of Fermoy, we were saluted with three cheers by Lieut. Colonel Stewart, (who was then commanding officer of the regiment), together with the

11

band and many of the old soldiers, who came to welcome us home. There we halted, and formed up into a line, that our colonel might see what sort of a bargain he had got; and after a little conversation with the officer that commanded our party, he walked up and down the ranks with a smiling countenance, accompanied by several other officers that belonged to the regiment.— Our party consisted of about four hundred, all young men. After a little rest, we marched off again, with drums beating and music playing, until we came to Fermoy barracks, and then we were divided as quick as possible, and sent to our respective companies: and for encouragement, our colonel had ordered a good dinner to be ready for us, which each company had placed on the table, together with a can of good porter, which you may suppose was very acceptable to us after a long days' march. Our dinner consisted of a piece of beef baked in the oven, with some potatoes; a leg of mutton, and a suet pudding boiled, with vegetables of all sorts that were needful, and a can of good porter as before mentioned. On the following day after being supplied with such articles as were necessary, we received the remainder of our bounty, and an order to go where we pleased for one week, to spend our money, and then to return to our barracks, and attend to our duty as soldiers ought to do. Having such liberty, you might suppose we did not forget to make the public houses rattle ; our liberty being up, and our money nearly all spent, we returned to our barracks according to order, and commenced our duty as soldiers once more.

Fermoy is not a large town, but cleaner than many other towns in general, and is situated close to the Black-water river; our barracks were very good, and stood on a hill very convenient to the town; so we remained there very comfortable till toward the latter end of November, when we received the route to march to Dublin. The first day we marched to Clogheen; the second, to Clonmell, (where our route was countermanded); and on the following, we marched to the city of Cashell. The barracks in that town were not large enough to take any more than two hundred men, but middling good; and, fortunately, our company was one that was put into them, for it was a most miserable dirty town, and very middling treatment among the inhabitants; their houses were in a very dirty state, in general, and the dress of most of the poor people appeared to me to agree very well with their houses; for I never saw any people so filthy, and untidy in their dress, in any other town that I was in: notwithstanding, one thing was much in our favour, provisions were very cheap; good beef at three-pence per ℔. and potatoes at two-pence-halfpenny the weight; (a weight is twenty-one ℔.) : so by living well, I did not much mind a few difficulties, and we did not remain there long.

For in the beginning of February, 1808, we received orders to march to Mallow, in the county of Cork; and the first day we marched to Clogheen for the third time; the second day, to Fermoy; and the third day, to Mallow barracks. There were small barracks in three different places in that town; but there was not room

13

enough, in all, to take the whole regiment. However, the people in that town were middling clean in general, and very agreeable, by which we made ourselves very comfortable. There was also a pleasant walk in this town which led to a hot well, that was surrounded by shady trees, (but there was no particular care taken of this well); and the river Black-water runs close by this town. Therefore, having nothing to do but our own regimental duty, we passed the time away very easy. However, our comfort did not continue many months, for toward the latter end of May, we received orders from government, to hold ourselves in readiness for foreign service; and in a short time after, orders came for embarkation, which put an end to all pleasure.

On the 16th of June, we marched to the city of Cork; the weather being then rather warm, we found it to be a very fatiguing day's march, being twenty-one Irish miles, (one Irish mile is a mile and a quarter English). The city of Cork is a much nobler place than the city of Waterford, and a great deal cleaner. On the following day, we marched to the Cove of Cork (which was about nine miles), and embarked the same day, in company with several other regiments.

We remained in the Cove till the 12th of July, 1808, waiting for more shipping and troops to join the fleet, as that was the place appointed for the expedition to assemble at: and as soon as all the fleet had arrived, and such arrangements made as were necessary, a signal was made for sailing; and on the 12th of July, 1808, we put to sea under the command of Sir Arthur

C

14

Wellesley, and about the middle of the day, the fleet were all out of the harbour, being about forty sail, when a signal was made from our commodore to make sail, and the fleet to keep as close together as possible, steering our course for the coast of Spain and Portugal. Our commodore was the Donegall, of 74 guns. The whole of this voyage proved very pleasant, having fine weather and such an easy sea; and to see such a quantity of fish alongside the ship, as there were sometimes, made it appear still more pleasant: some appeared to our view to be five or six feet in length. We continued sailing with a steady breeze until about the 25th, when the weather being clear, we discovered land on our larboard side, which proved to be some part of Spain. We did not put into any port in Spain, but continued along the coast to Portugal; and on the 29th of July, we came to an anchor in Mondego Bay, and expected to land immediately; however, we remained on board until the 2d of August, and soon after sun rise, that morning, a signal was made to disembark: therefore, as soon as we were supplied with three day's provision, which was done without delay, we proceeded towards the shore. When the Portuguese understood that we were their protectors, they came flocking down on the beach in droves; and there being no convenience for landing, without getting into the water, the Portuguese men came running into the water, above their knees, to carry us out of the boats; and what made it still more pleasing to us, the young women came flocking around us, with their aprons full of fruit; some with oranges, some with

15

grapes, and some with figs, &c. crying, "*Veavo, veavo, Englees!*" that is, "*Long live the English!*" It being so warm in that country, at that time of the year, the men had not much trouble in taking off their clothes to carry us out of the boats; for the manner of dress of the poor people, along the sea coast, is a sort of sleeved waistcoat, very seldom buttoned, with a pair of linen drawers of a very large size, which reach a little below the knee, without button or string at the knee, which they can turn up without any difficulty, should they want to wade through a stream of water: neither do they wear any stockings, and many are without shoes; but some wear a sort of clogs that are very thick and clumsy; their hats are very broad but shallow, much resembling a shepherd's hat in this country. The women wear neither hat, cap, or bonnet; but generally a white handkerchief thrown over their heads, and pinned under the chin, with the corners hanging carelessly down the bosom; and many of the poor women are without stockings in the summer, in the country places; but the people in Lisbon, and other large towns, are rather more genteel in their dress, in particular the women, about their feet and legs, who generally wear white cotton stockings, and very neatly made shoes of many colours. The poor people have in general a chain of beads placed round the neck, which hangs down the breast, with a cross at the bottom; these beads they make use of instead of a prayer book, by way of telling them over and over.

We all made our landing good, excepting one boat load of the 45th regiment of foot, which was upset by

C 2

the violence of such a heavy swell, in crossing the bar at
the mouth of the river Mondego, and unfortunately,
several soldiers and sailors were drowned. The bar is
a sort of quicksand that is always in confusion, and
rises nearly to the surface of the water, which causes
great danger in crossing. As soon as all were landed,
we proceeded about nine miles towards Lisbon, without
any opposition, to a place called Lavos, and there we
encamped on a sort of a woody common, without tents
or blankets; but every man had a watch coat, and there
being such a quantity of myrtle bushes on our camp
ground, we set to work, and gathered a parcel together,
which made us a comfortable bed. There we remained until the 9th of August, by which time every
necessary arrangement was made, when we received orders to proceed in pursuit of the enemy.

Being supplied with three days' provisions, we
commenced our march, taking our direction through
Leyria, towards Lisbon, in which direction the enemy
lay. Leyria was the first town that we marched through,
which place the enemy left in a wretched condition:
many houses were on fire when we entered the town,
and many others were very much damaged, and the
furniture beat to pieces in a frightful manner; the
inhabitants were also treated very ill, the women in
particular.

The light brigade pursued the enemy very close
from this town, and some skirmishing took place; but
our brigade continued its march, without opposition, till
the 15th, when a party of Portuguese came running to

17

our commander, to inform him, that a plundering party of the French was in Nazaret, a small town about two leagues to our right, on the sea coast. Sir Arthur Wellesley having this intelligence, immediately despatched our light company and a troop of the 20th light dragoons in pursuit of them with all possible speed; and when we came within about a mile of the town, we saw a great smoke ascending: we were then ordered to load, expecting to have something to do very soon. However, when we came there, we found the enemy had evacuated the town, and destroyed it nearly all, by fire; and to the great misfortune of the poor inhabitants, what provisions they could not take away, they destroyed, the wine in particular, for they even beat the barrels to pieces: so all that the inhabitants could accommodate us with, was fruit out of the fields, which they brought to us in abundance.

Being very much fatigued, we remained there that night; and in the evening, just as we were thinking to lay ourselves down to get a little rest, we were alarmed by a party of the inhabitants, who were coming running towards us with shouts of joy, and loaded with pans and pitchers full of wine, that they had found in some part of the town, in a place that the enemy did not happen to find: so they all sat down with us, and we enjoyed ourselves with fruit and wine as long as we thought proper: and as we did not understand their language, nor they ours, we drank health to each other by motions. Next morning, we proceeded on our march to join the army again; and as the weather was very warm, we found it to be a

C 3

18

very fatiguing day's march, (being from break of day in the morning, till sun-set in the evening), and a great part of the road was very sandy, some times sinking nearly ancle deep in sand. When we came up with the regiment, we found a party of another company cooking our provisions for us, which was a very pleasing sight after a long fatiguing day's march. Having nothing more to do that night, but to sit down and fill our bellies, and then lie down to rest, as soon as we had eaten our suppers, we wrapped ourselves up in our watch coats, and lay down among some bushes, near Obidos.

On the following morning, being the 17th day of August, 1808, about six o'clock, we were alarmed by a sharp firing of musketry, which proved to be with the out-lying piquets and the enemy: in consequence of which, we immediately stood to our arms, and proceeded towards the heights of Rolea, on which place a sharp engagement took place; for the main body of the enemy had formed on those heights. Some skirmishing had taken place before we came to the heights; for they had several skirmishing parties formed in the olive orchards, in order to check our advance; but the light companies of the different regiments soon scoured them out. Between Obidos and Rolea, is a plain fruitful bit of land, mostly gardens and orchards for several miles, some vineyards, and almost surrounded with hills. While driving the enemy's skirmishers, our company passed through one garden, in particular, that was all onions, (at least, I could see nothing else), which I considered to be nearly two acres, and several other smaller gardens that were filled with pumpkins and melons, with some fruit trees, besides olive orchards. The weather being so warm, and water not convenient, a little fruit would have been very acceptable; but as we advanced so rapidly, we could only snatch an apple or a bunch of grapes as we passed along.

The main body of the enemy having placed themselves on the heights, was a great disadvantage to us; for as soon as we approached within cannon shot distance, they began to throw cannon shot among us; and when we came to the hill, we found great difficulty in some places in ascending, being obliged to pull ourselves up by some bushes or tufts of grass; at the same time they continued pouring down musket shot on us very sharply.

The 29th regiment being about a quarter of a mile on our left, and having some little better road than our regiment, they ascended the heights a few minutes before us; upon which, the enemy immediately attacked them with a much superior force, and caused them to fall back with the loss of their colours, and about three hundred men: but as soon as we made our appearance on the top of the heights, it was a great relief to them: and the first thing our colonel thought most proper to do, was to show them the point of the bayonet, which we immediately did; and much to their shame and disgrace, we drove them off the heights in a few minutes; at the same time the remains of the 29th regiment gave them another grand charge, by which they retook their colours and some prisoners. But unfortunately, in this attack Lieut. Colonel Stewart, who commanded the 9th regiment, was killed; and also, the colonel of the 29th. The enemy fell back a little distance, and then turned and attacked us again; but was received most gallantly, and soon repulsed. They afterwards made several attacks upon our regiment and the 29th, before any other regiment came up to our assistance, but without effect, as they found true Englishmen every time; and it is certain, that the 9th and 29th regiments were exposed to nearly all the French army for some time: but when some other regiments came up we obliged them to retreat; and soon after they began to feel the effects of a few cannon shot, and some shells, they retreated very rapidly. As it was thought not proper to advance any further that day, we kept our ground, which put an end to the action; and about four or five o'clock in the afternoon, there was silence on both sides.

As soon as our camp was formed, some immediately set to work, gathering the wounded together, and conveying them to Obidos; while another party was busy in burying the dead. The loss of our regiment, on this occasion, consisted of our colonel, killed; our first major, wounded; and our second major dismounted, (in consequence of having his horse killed); one captain, and two lieutenants, wounded; and nearly one hundred brave soldiers killed and wounded. After our wounded were secured, and the dead buried, we sat ourselves down in order to get a little refreshment, and in a short time night began to approach; upon which, we

21

laid ourselves down among the bushes, to get a little
rest.

On the following morning, we proceeded on our
advance in pursuit of the enemy, as usual; and on the
20th, we took up our position on some hills near
Vimiera, where Sir Arthur thought it most proper to
make another attack, should the enemy be that way
inclined; for their whole force had joined together at
a short distance from this place. Next morning, being
Sunday, the 21st of August, we stood to our arms
before break of day, and every arrangement was made
for the attack, should the enemy advance. We remained under arms nearly two hours after day-light; but as
they did not approach, and every thing seemed quiet,
orders were given to lodge our arms, and prepare for
cooking, in the usual manner: and in a short time, some
were busily employed in washing their shirts, being a
very convenient place for that purpose, (for there was
a small river ran very near our camp, and also plenty of
wood for cooking): but, to our surprise, when just in
the midst of our washing and other camp employments,
the enemy began to approach, and made an attack on
two or three brigades, quite unawares. But as English
courage is not so easily daunted, we were all under arms,
and ready for action, almost in one minute; and such
regiments as were attacked so suddenly, were engaged,
very sharp, in an instant, and did not forget to pay the
enemy for so daring an assault. As it is not English
fashion to play at ball long, if there is a possibility of
giving a charge, so likewise, at this time we soon pre-

sented them the point of the bayonet, and gave them a
charge that was not acceptable; for they soon turned
about, and made off as well as they could, but not without great loss. Several other brigades were soon engaged very sharply; but at length, the enemy was
repulsed and driven in all directions.

This action did not continue much more than three
hours; for just in the midst of our glory, we were
ordered to halt, and were not permitted to advance any
more that day, which caused a great murmuring among
the army, in particular in such regiments as had not
been engaged; for every soldier seemed anxious to push
on, as we could plainly see that a great part of the
French army would have been our prisoners, (or otherwise there must have been great slaughter among
them), had we been permitted to continue our advance;
for ten or twelve pieces of cannon and many ammunition
waggons had already fallen into our hands, as also
many prisoners, though several regiments had not fired
a shot; however, our whole brigade, which formed the
reserve under the command of General Hill, was not
brought into action.

As Sir Arthur Wellesley was riding up and down in
front of our brigade, the men loudly called out to him,
from one end of the line to the other, saying, " Let us
" advance! let us advance! the enemy is in great
" confusion!" but his answer was, " I have nothing
" to do with it—I have no command." We were as-
tonished to hear him say, " I have no command:" and
in a short time, instead of advancing, we were ordered

23

to take up our former position; and soon after, it was
reported among us, that he was superseded in the command by another general, when in the midst of the
engagement; and we had every reason to believe, that
was the reason why we were not permitted to continue
our advance. So about one or two o'clock in the afternoon, the enemy having quite left the field, we recommenced our cookery as before, and remained very quiet
the rest of that day: and on the following day we
understood that a *Rimple* had sprung up.

In the course of this day, Junot, who commanded
the French army, sent a flag of truce, requesting the
liberty to quit Portugal with the honours of war. His
proposals were, that the French army should embark
in the river Tagus, and that every man should take his
arms, accoutrements, and sixty rounds of amunition with
him; and also, all private and public baggage; and that
they should be disembarked in France. All these proposals were agreed to; which caused a much greater
murmuring than was on the 21st, for no one ever
thought a *Rimple* would have caused such a contrast.
When those arrangements were settled, the French
army embarked on board of English shipping, with
colours flying and music playing, all the men loaded
like bees, with the plunder of the country; which was
enough to make us do what the laws of our country will
not allow; for all this plunder would certainly have
fallen into our hands, had not there been such a *Rimple*.

The enemy having evacuated the country, our
camp was formed within about two leagues of Lisbon,

and Sir Arthur Wellesley returned to England on some particular business; and in a short time, that *Rimple,* who had caused so much discontent, was recalled. So now having nothing in particular to do, and being settled at camp, we were soon provided with good tents, in order to shade us from the scorching sun in the day, and also from the heavy dews of the night. Here we remained nearly two months, and in the course of that time, Lieutenant General Sir John Moore arrived, and took the command of the army; and in consequence of the French having possession of some parts in Spain, we received orders to proceed to that country, in order to try our skill there. Therefore, towards the latter end of October, we commenced our march for Salamanca, in Spain, (making regular stages), and took up our quarters in the different towns or villages every night. We took our direction about three leagues to the left of Santarem, through Leyria, to Coimbra; and from thence by Guarda, (leaving it about two leagues to our right), through Celorico, and close by Almeida, to St. Felices, which was the first town that we entered in Spain; and about the middle of November, we arrived at Salamanca, after a march of nearly three hundred miles, and great part of the way the weather and roads were very bad. After such a long fatiguing march, and being not many leagues from the enemy, General Moore thought it necessary to halt awhile, in order to get a little rest, and also to wait the arrival of more troops that were coming to join our army.

25

Salamanca is a very large town, situated about thirty leagues from Madrid, with mostly strong stone buildings. There are many large convents in that town, several very fine squares, and a regular market every day, except Sunday, where you might purchase any thing that the country produces. The inhabitants seemed very friendly, more so than in many other places; for in several towns in Spain, the inhabitants have even barred their doors against us, and we have been obliged to beat them open with our muskets, before we could get entrance. However, being now in a plentiful and friendly place, and having five months' arrears of pay due to us, we all seemed anxious to have a little advanced, in order to purchase some few articles that we might stand in need of, and also, a few bottles of wine, to enjoy ourselves a little before we advanced any further. As our commanding officer would not advance any money, we passed the word to Sir John Moore, upon which our request was immediately granted; and an order was given, that every man should be paid all his demands, except ten shillings, which sum should be kept in hand in order to purchase such articles as in a little time we might stand in need of. Now, after having a few days' rest, and a few bottles of good wine, we recommenced our advance in good spirits, and continued about one hundred and fifty miles further, (where we expected the Spanish army would join), taking our direction from Salamanca through Ledesma to Zamora, and from thence to Sahagun, leaving Benevento about four or five leagues on our left.

D

26

Being now within three leagues of the enemy, we were alarmed, about seven o'clock in the evening of the 23d of December, by the sound of our bugles, to stand to our arms, in order to proceed two leagues nearer to him that night. When we were assembled, we commenced our march according to orders; but in consequence of the ground being covered with a deep snow, we had some difficulty in finding our road. However, some time after the middle of the night, we arrived at the place appointed, and when our line was formed, and our piquets posted, we were allowed to break off and walk up and down, with particular orders not to make any noise: but being rather fatigued, some scraped the snow away, and sat down in order to rest their legs a little; but we were not permitted even to take off our knapsacks, neither to put down our arms, (for our piquets and the enemy's were almost within gun shot of each other), and we were ordered to examine our flints, and see that they were in good order, and undoubtedly every good soldier would always be prepared with a good flint, if there was a possibility.

Now, what could we expect when day-light did appear ?—why to combat our enemy, as you might suppose: but we had not been sitting much more than half an hour, when our officers came whispering to us, to stand to our arms, and not to speak a word; and to our great surprise, we found that an express had arrived from the commander of the Spanish army, saying that their army was not fit for the field, neither could they join; at least it was so reported among us. Now what a contrast was here: no honour had we gained, and the enemy about three to one: all that we could do, was to turn our backs to them, and get away in the best manner we could.

So about three or four o'clock in the morning of the 24th of December, 1808, we commenced our retreat towards Corunna, that being the place appointed by Sir John Moore for our army to embark at. You may easily suppose this was rather teazing, having already marched between four and five hundred miles since October, and had now nearly three hundred more to march before there were any hopes of getting some rest, supposing I should be so fortunate as to reach Corunna safe, as by the help of God I did, though many a hundred brave soldiers were not so fortunate. Having commenced our retreat, we took our direction through Benevento, near which place we blew up the bridge, in order to check the enemy's advance; and two or three other bridges were also blown up on our retreat. But in spite of all, the enemy's cavalry were, in general, close to our heels; by which some skirmishing took place with our cavalry and theirs every day. From Benevento, we marched through Astorga and Villa Franca, to Lugo, (which is a large town about eighteen leagues from Corunna), not halting more than four or five hours in one place, till we arrived at Lugo.

By this time, a number of the army were almost bare-footed; for the weather and the roads had been very bad most of the way, which caused the men to straggle, and many brave soldiers had already fallen.

into the hands of the enemy, in consequence of the same: therefore, General Moore thought it necessary to make a stand at this place, in order to gather the stragglers together, that they might join their respective regiments; and also, to get such men as were quite barefooted a little forward. As for stores, we had but little; for in consequence of the enemy advancing so rapidly, we were obliged to destroy the greater part of them, and an immense quantity of ammunition; for our cattle had got so weak, for want of forage and rest, that they could not be got along by any means whatever; and we were obliged even to leave our money behind. In one place, the money barrels were placed on the brink of a hill, just by the road side, and rolled down the hill: and we being pursued so closely, some of it was left in the road. Perhaps, some might be ready to ask, why was not this money delivered out to the army?—why, had that been the case, it is most likely it would have caused great irregularity; the reason why is this: being fatigued and very hungry, (as certainly we were), some would have straggled off the road, to the different villages, in order to purchase bread and wine, by which means there is no doubt but many more would have fallen into the hands of the enemy; therefore, we might consider it best as it was

We halted at Lugo two days, where, of course, it was necessary to form ourselves into a position of defence. However, the main body of the enemy did not advance upon us so rapidly as we expected; therefore,

we did not come to a general engagement, as only three
or four regiments, on the left of our line, (that fell in
with them) were engaged for about two hours. Neither
was there a general engagement during the retreat; but
of a truth, there was skirmishing nearly every day with
our rear guard and the enemy's advance.

Having now formed ourselves in readiness to receive the enemy, the next thing that we stood most in
need of, was something to satisfy hunger; so during the
time we halted here, the commissary delivered out to
us, one day's allowance of rum, (which is a quart between six men), and as no bread could be got for love
or money, the commissary delivered out one pound of
flour to each man, which was happily accepted, for at
that time we were very hungry; and now we were
all for the quickest way of making it ready for eating,
some making it into small cakes, and baking them on
the fire coals; and others making it into spoon-victuals.
After having this little refreshment, and night coming
on, we laid ourselves down on the wet ground, in
hopes of getting a little rest, placing our heads on our
knapsacks, which we generally did, that being something softer than a stone; but in consequence of the wind
and rain, our rest was but middling, although we were
not disturbed by the enemy that night.

On the following day, orders were given to gather
a parcel of wood together, in order to make some large
fires in the evening; so ten men from each company were
immediately warned for that purpose, and in consequence of wood being so scarce, or, as I might say,

D 3

none convenient to our camp, they were ordered to pull down some old houses that were pointed out to them, and to make use of the timber for the fires. These orders were soon put into execution; but in consequence of the rain, we had great difficulty in making our fires: however, about six o'clock in the evening, we had some very comfortable fires, and we all placed ourselves around them as comfortable as our situation would allow: but at that time we were in a miserable dirty condition, not having our clothes off for about six weeks.

However, we did not enjoy our fires long; for between seven and eight o'clock, our officers came whispering to us, to stand to our arms, and not to speak a a word: so in a few minutes, we were on our line of march again, muddling through the rain and dirt. It being so very dark, and the roads so deep, you may suppose we had very uncomfortable marching: but to banter the enemy a little, two men from each company were left behind for about half an hour, for the purpose of keeping the fires good, but not to stay longer than half an hour, and then to make the best of their way after the army: but nevertheless, at day-light in the morning, the enemy's advance guard was close to our heels, as usual. We continued creeping along till about four o'clock in the afternoon, when we came to a town, (the name I cannot remember), and in consequence of such a heavy fall of rain, we received orders to halt for a few hours, in order to gather the stragglers; for during the last twenty hours, we had left more than half of our men behind. Luckily, here we found one of our commissaries, with some liquors, but neither bread nor meat; for bread had been a very scarce thing all through the retreat; however, we found a drop of good rum very acceptable, to keep the cold out of our insides, for we were very wet. As soon as we had got this drop of rum, (which we waited for more than an hour in the rain), we were ordered to go and make our quarters good where we could, and to be ready at a minute's warning: so having these orders, we dispersed for a short time, some going to one house and some to another.

But before we could hardly make our quarters good, the bugles were sounding in all parts of the town, and some dragoons were firing their pistols in the streets, in order to make the alarm as quick as possible; for the enemy had driven our rear guard to within one mile of the town; but by the great exertions of our dragoons, was obliged to retreat again: therefore we escaped all danger that time. Being assembled again in this miserable condition, wet, hungry, and fatigued as we were, we started again, the wind blowing hard and the rain pouring, and it likewise getting very dark, being between six and seven o'clock in the evening; and what made it still more aggravating, in a very little time I had lost one of my shoes, which caused my eyes to flow with tears, and those of many other brave soldiers that were in the same condition. Nevertheless, we continued moving on, very slowly, until the evening of the following day, not halting more than a quarter of an hour in one place, when we came to Betanzos. Before we entered the town, we were halted, in order to march regularly through; but when we assembled all hands, our regiment did not exceed sixty men; neither did any regiment in the brigade exceed that number; however, the whole brigade could not muster two hundred and fifty men. It consisted of the 9th, 23d, 43d, and 52d regiments of foot.

After a few minutes rest, we proceeded through the town, but instead of continuing on our march, as we expected, being only three leagues from Corunna, we were put into a chapel which was close to the road side, and remained there till day-light in the morning, in order to gather as many of the stragglers together as might be able to come on. During this miserable retreat, from Lugo to this place, we lost between three and four hundred men of our regiment, merely with fatigue and hunger, who fell into the hands of the enemy; and it is certain, that some few individuals were seen to breathe their last on the road side. There is one thing more that I cannot help mentioning, which was a most melancholy scene: that was, an English woman, one of our soldiers' wives, lying dead on the road side, with a young child sucking at the breast, and, to all appearance, likely to survive if taken care of: but what became of the woman's husband, or what regiment he belonged to, I cannot ascertain.

The last day of our retreat, which was the 15th of January, 1809, we hove in sight of Corunna, which was a joyful sight to us, having a view of all the shipping

that was waiting to receive us; and for joy that we were
going to retire to our own native country once more, our
fatigue was soon smothered with songs, although not
hardly able to crawl along the road.   About the middle
of the day, we entered Corunna, (a large garrison town)
and were put into a convent.   In the afternoon, we were
accommodated with plenty of good bread and wine,
which was provided by the Spaniards; and salt beef and
pork, that were brought from on board our shipping.

In this place, the Spaniards were very friendly,
and likewise exerted themselves in a soldier-like manner,
by giving us all the assistance that they possibly could.
So, having plenty of good bread, meat, and wine, we
made ourselves very comfortable that night; and the
same evening, some few individuals were presented with
a pair of shoes.   In consequence of the garrison being
so much out of repair, we were put to work the following morning, repairing the ramparts and batteries;
and having a belly-full of good victuals and drink,
we continued our work, as well as our strength would
allow, until about the middle of the day, when we were
alarmed by a sharp firing of musketry between our out-
piquets and the enemy.   This caused our work to be
immediately put aside, and we were ordered to stand to
our arms as quick as possible, and proceed to the alarm
post.   In a few minutes we were all ready for action,
except the sick, and some that were lame in consequence
of having no shoes: which men were ordered to be put
on board immediately.

Now being assembled, we marched out of the town about two miles, where a sharp engagement soon took place, and continued till it was quite dark, when the enemy retreated. In this engagement, several regiments suffered very severely; likewise, Lieut. Gen. Sir John Moore received his fatal wound on this day, which was the 16th of January, 1809. However, it did not fall to our lot to partake of this action, neither did any of our brigade fall in with them: nevertheless we were within call during the whole time, expecting to be summoned up every minute. About nine o'clock in the evening, having gathered the wounded together, we retreated back to the town again, and took up our quarters as before, and on the following morning our army began to embark: but in consequence of our brigade not having a share in the action the day before, we were detained on shore, in order to cover the embarkation: we therefore kept possession of the town until about eight o'clock in the evening, when we delivered up the gates to the Spaniards, and proceeded to the place appointed for embarkation.

In the afternoon of this day, the enemy placed a brigade of guns on the top of the hill, (undiscovered by us), which they brought to bear upon the shipping, and upon that part of the town that our regiment was in, (which lay very convenient to the harbour), for several shots passed through the roof of the house we were in: but Providence smiled on us this time; for not a man received any injury. However, this bit of an alarm put our transport sailors in such confusion, that several of them cut their cables and left their anchors behind; in consequence of which, in a few minutes, many of them were so entangled, one among the other, that two very fine ships were run aground and were not able to float any more. It being very dark, these two ships were set on fire, which made a most excellent light for us to embark by; and at about ten o'clock, just as we were in the act of getting into our boats, a crowd of Spaniards came running, almost out of breath, to inform us, that there were three large houses left full of wounded English soldiers. Upon this intelligence, twenty men from the right of our company, and twenty from another company, (accompanied by General Beresford and his staff), were detained on shore for the purpose of getting the wounded men on board. This task was a very fatiguing one; being full a quarter of a mile to carry the men, and having no convenience for so doing, except on our backs, or in blankets, which was very uneasy carriage for us, and worse for the wounded; for the cries and groans of some of these poor men were enough to pierce the heart of a stone; and not only that, for the enemy continued throwing cannon shot and shells into the town during the whole night: but the Almighty so ordered it, that we received no harm. Thus having secured our wounded comrades, the next thing to do, was to secure ourselves: but having a distance of nearly three miles to go in the open boats, it being very dark, and the wind blowing very hard, made it appear very unpleasant: but to avoid any difficulty in finding our way, a light was placed in the rigging of the ship, (which was the Audacious, of 74 guns), and at about four o'clock in the morning of the 18th of January, 1809, we all got safe on board; and as soon as all was secure, orders were given to weigh anchor and put to sea, which were soon put into execution.

The wind still continued blowing very hard, which carried us, the whole of the following day, about thirteen knots an hour; and after a few hours' rest, I employed myself in repairing my old clothes. I always carried needles and thread about with me, as soldiers in general do, but not being able to procure patches of the colour of my clothes, I was obliged to content myself with some pieces of old sack bagging. We continued on our course, crowding all the sail we possibly could carry, until the 24th in the evening, when we came to an anchor at Spithead; and on the following day, a signal was made for us to re-embark on board a transport ship, which was lying at anchor in Portsmouth harbour, in order to go by water round to Dover, which was only one day's march from Canterbury, that being the depot for our regiment at that time: for in our present dirty ragged condition, we were not fit to march through a clean Christian country. However, during the time we remained on board, we employed ourselves in cleaning our old clothes and appointments, which made us appear a little more like soldiers. In consequence of a contrary wind, we remained in the harbour until the 28th, when a signal was made to un-

37.

moor and put to sea; but there being such a quantity of shipping in the harbour, night began to approach before we could hardly clear it. Therefore, the captain of the ship thought it necessary to drop our anchor, just at the entrance of the harbour, intending to remain there till day-light. But a little before the middle of the night, we were suddenly alarmed by a tremendous gale of wind, which caused our ship to drag her anchor; and had it not been for the great exertions of the sailors, and a little assistance from some of our soldiers, we certainly must have been cast away; for it would have been almost impossible for any boats to have come to our assistance: but by throwing out three anchors, we escaped. Nevertheless, at day-light next morning, we found ourselves within two hundred yards of the shore, having dragged our anchors nearly a quarter of a mile; and had likewise four feet of water in the hold: for by the violence of the wind, and such a rough sea, the ship had sprung a leak. About sun-rising, the wind abated, when we put back into harbour as quick as possible.

In consequence of the ship being rendered unfit for sea, and the weather so unfavourable, orders came to disembark, which we did in the afternoon of the 29th of January, 1809, at Gosport, and were put into barracks for that night, where we formed a party, consisting of two lieutenants, our sergeant major (with the colours), four sergeants, one drum, and about one hundred and fifty men. On the following day, we commenced our march for Canterbury; and on the 30th of January, we marched to Fareham; the 31st, to Wickham; the

E

1st of February, to. Alton; and the 2d, to Farnham.
In this town, the street was crowded with the inhabitants, and as soon as we halted to receive our billets,
the people came flocking round us with pots of beer,
saying, " Drink, soldiers! for several parties have
" marched through this town, but not one appeared so
" clean and soldier-like as this party.' And for encouragement, some gentlemen walked round to the different
public houses in the evening, and ordered each man a
quart of strong beer. On the 3d, we marched to Guil-
ford; the 4th, we halted; the 5th, to Dorking; the
6th, to Sevenoaks; the 7th, to Maidstone; the 8th, to
————; and the 9th, to the city of Canterbury.

Here we found about fifty men of our regiment,
in possession of the new barracks, who had arrived
several days before us from Dover; for in consequence
of being a few in one ship, and a few in another, some
disembarked at Plymouth, some at Gosport, some at
Dover, and some at Liverpool. Therefore, about the
end of February, we assembled about four hundred and
fifty men: but when we disembarked in Portugal, our
strength was one thousand and twenty men. Having
now good comfortable barracks, clean bedding, and
good living, the next thing that we stood most in need
of, was clothing; which we were supplied with, from
head to foot, as soon as possibly it could be procured;
and the whole of the old was committed to the fire.
In a very little time we were very comfortably situated;
having very moderate duty, and being treated by
the inhabitants with friendship: notwithstanding, one

thing was still rather alarming among us, and that was, a very strong fever, by which many a brave soldier was summoned to his last home. However, by medical assistance, the disorder abated in a few weeks.

In consequence of losing so many men on this sad retreat, another order was given out from government, for a general volunteering from the militia, to replace those that were missing, (there being another grand expedition wanted toward the north, as soon as possible): therefore, in the month of April, about five hundred fine young men joined us, who had volunteered from the militia; and, to my great surprize, among this party I found my brother, who had volunteered from the North Gloucester Militia, having enlisted to serve his Majesty in that regiment about the same time that I volunteered my service into the 9th. My brother being so tall, he was immediately pointed out to join the grenadier company; therefore, we could not have the happiness of being both in the same company, for I had always been in the light company.

Perhaps, some will be ready to ask, What difference is there in these two companies?—Why, the grenadier company consists of all the tallest and stoutest men in the regiment, and always stands on the right; but the light company is generally young men, straight and slender, (who stand from about five feet seven to five feet nine inches high), and when in settled quarters, stands on the left of the regiment; but on the line of march, they are placed several hundred yards in front, as a sort of advance guard; that if the enemy

E 2

should make an attack, they may be immediately extended at such a distance from each file, as would about cover the regiment when in line. They then commence independent firing; but not without signal, which is made by the sound of the bugle, (for on such occasions as these, the light company does all its motions by the sound of the bugle), and as soon as the regiment is formed up, they retreat to the line in double-quick time.

So, by having this party of volunteers from the militia, and a few more old hands that joined from different hospitals, our regiment mustered nearly one thousand strong, well clothed, and in good health; in consequence of which, we were soon summoned to hold ourselves in readiness for foreign service again; and on the 17th of July, 1809, at five o'clock in the morning, we assembled in the barrack yard, in marching order, to march to Deal, as the expedition was to assemble in the Downs. But in consequence of some misconduct of two men the night before, instead of marching off in the usual way, we were formed into square, and a drum-head court martial ordered to sit immediately, for the trial of the two men, who bore but a middling character in general. So according to order, they were tried, and sentenced to receive two hundred lashes in the usual manner. But that they should not escape going on this expedition, the colonel mitigated the punishment, by giving them only one hundred lashes each, and to be marched as prisoners with the baggage. This being done, we marched off about seven o'clock, with drums beating and colours flying, through the city:

41

and being so united with the inhabitants, the streets were crowded with people who were waiting to bid us farewell; as also many young women with watery eyes, who were then deprived of their fancy men.

Being heavy loaded, and the weather very warm, we continued moving along very slowly until about two o'clock, when we arrived at Deal, which was nineteen miles; but instead of being put into quarters for that night, as we expected to be, we were marched down to the place of embarkation, and put on board immediately: eight companies on board two transport ships, and the grenadier and light company on board the Thalia frigate, accompanied with the band and the staff of the regiment.

The Downs being the place appointed for the fleet to assemble at, we remained there several days, waiting for more troops, &c. and when the whole fleet was assembled, (which consisted of between two and three hundred sail), it appeared at distance, or, as I might say, to people standing on the shore, something resembling a wood. This was the finest expedition ever known to sail from England. On the 29th, a signal was made to put to sea; and in a short time the shore was crowded with people, who came to take a view of the fleet; for when in full sail, is was a most beautiful sight; and as soon as all were under weigh, a signal was made to make sail and to keep as close together as possible. We steered our course for the Island of Walcheren, being led on by ten sail of the line, besides frigates and other small craft.

42

We continued sailing with a pleasant breeze until the following morning, when we hove in sight of our destination, and towards the evening, came to an anchor very convenient to the shore, alongside the mainland of Holland, and likewise the island of Walcheren; for it is only a river that divides this island from the main continent.

Next morning, a signal was made to disembark; and being supplied with three days' provisions, (which was done without delay), we were ordered into the boats. Our regiment and several others were ordered to proceed towards the main land, in order to make an attack there; at the same time, the other part of the army was to make an attack on the Island of Walcheren; but we had not got many yards towards the shore, when a signal was made for our regiment and all others that were steering for the main land, to re-embark till further orders. But the other part of the army continued steering for the island, and made a grand attack: the enemy made a strong opposition, having several batteries close to the sea side: nevertheless, in a short time the batteries were in our possession, and British colours placed thereon. According to English fashion, as soon as we could form up into line, we gave them a volley, and then three cheers and a charge, which put them into such confusion, that they began to run towards the town of Flushing something like a flock of sheep driven by the shepherd's dog. As they would not accept of the bayonet, we obliged them to accept of a few pills, by which many of them fell asleep. Our loss in making our landing good, was but trifling.

On the following morning, being the 1st of August, a signal was made for the remaining part of the army to disembark on the island of South Beveland, which was very convenient to the island of Walcheren. All being ready, and waiting for the signal, we were immediately ordered into the boats, and proceeded towards that island, expecting to have a warm breakfast; but, fortunately, we made our landing good without opposition; for the enemy had evacuated the island in the night. There being several towns and villages on the island, the different regiments were soon separated, some going one road and some another, towards their respective quarters, which were pointed out to them: our regiment occupied two villages, the right wing at ————, and the left wing at St. Herenshock. In this village our company took up their quarters in a small chapel; and the others, in the barns that were most convenient to the village. The inhabitants showed us every mark of friendship, by giving us vegetables of every sort that the island did produce, which were much the same as in England. This island is about nine miles across: a great part of it lies very low, and is generally covered with water in the wet season; in consequence of which, the main roads are thrown up eight or ten feet above the surface of the land. Here we had our provisions very regularly; and likewise, some fatigue: for in consequence of there being so many ditches, (that were made to lead the water off the land), we were ordered out most days, in order to practise jumping these ditches; that if the enemy should make an attack on the island, we should not be unacquainted with jumping. But, however, we were not alarmed by the enemy during the time that we remained on the island.

The troops that were on the island of Walcheren were very busily employed, day and night, making batteries and breast-works round the town of Flushing; for in consequence of their fortifications being so strong, there was no possibility of taking the town by storm, without the loss of an immense number of men; therefore, the only method that we could take, to get possession of the town, was to batter it down by a heavy cannonading, or by setting fire to it; both of which were done, but not without the loss of a great number of brave British soldiers: for the whole time that our works were being carried on, the enemy kept up a continual fire, with shot and shells, day and night; and sometimes destroyed as much of our works in one day, as we could repair in a whole night. But, however, as soon as our works were completed, we did not forget to let them feel the effects of our bull-dogs; at the same time throwing a quantity of Congreve rockets into the town, which would burn with such fury, that the water engines were totally useless: therefore, in a short time several parts of the town were in a blaze of fire, and tumbling about in all quarters. In consequence of this, the enemy was obliged to surrender; for the town was so guarded by our shipping, that there was no possibility of making their escape: so having surrendered themselves prisoners of war, they were immediately conveyed to England.

When we entered the town, it was a most frightful place to behold; for many of their dead were then lying in the streets; and some of the inhabitants, who had not left the town, were walking about in a miserable condition, with their faces and heads cut and bruised in a frightful manner, which appeared to have been done by some pieces of slates or splinters falling from the buildings. Some of the houses that were standing, appeared to be in a very dangerous state, and likewise the church and tower were very much damaged by our shot. The principal thing that was found in this town, was saltpetre, of which were several hundred tons, and being a very useful thing in time of war, it was put on board as soon as possible, and likewise all other stores that were of any consequence.

This being done, our stay here was very short; for in the beginning of September, we received orders to quit these two islands, and return to England: and not much too soon; for our army began to fall down very fast with sickness, and the enemy advancing with a very powerful army, which had assembled on the continent, and being only a river that divided these two islands from the main continent, the enemy began to approach on the island of South Beveland before we could hardly make a shift to get out: for as there was a boat or two more than was wanted to take us on board, a boat's crew stepped on shore, and ran into a village in order to purchase something to drink; but they had not been there many minutes, before they were surprised by a party of French rifle-men, which pursued them so close, that they were obliged to give themselves up as prisoners of war.

Now our army being on board, a signal was made to put to sea and steer for the Downs; therefore, we immediately put to sea with a fair wind, crowding all sail that was needful until the next day, when we came to an anchor in the Downs; and on the following morning, being the 17th of September, 1809, we disembarked at Deal, and marched to Canterbury again for a little time. When we came to the entrance of the town, we beheld the streets crowded with people, who had been previously informed by a party that was sent forward on some necessary duty, that we were on the road, and about what time we should arrive: so we were received with shouts of joy; and the young women that we had left behind with watery eyes, were then gazing on us with smiling countenances. We took possession of the new barracks, as before: but in a short time our hospital was crowded with sick: every day the number of the sick increased with the ague and fever, for in about one month, nearly half our regiment was on the sick list, by which a great many were summoned to their last homes. Several times, three or four in a day were carried to the burial ground; and there were but few in the regiment that escaped having the ague either sooner or later.

We did not remain at Canterbury quite six months, when to our surprise, we received an order from goternment, for foreign service again, which was rather mortifying to us: some compared it to cock-fighting, for a good game cock may come off victorious in several battles, but the case is, in general, that he is tried over and over again, until he is either killed or disabled: so likewise, was the case with us; for on the 3d of March, 1810, we assembled, in marching order, about eight hundred strong, leaving about one hundred behind, that had not recovered from their sickness. So we marched off in the usual manner, with drums beating and colours flying, through the city, for Ramsgate. I think it needless to say much about our departure this time; only, that if it seemed hard parting when we marched off for Flushing, it now appeared to be a great deal worse.

Having arrived at Ramsgate, we embarked immediately on board three transport ships, and on the following morning, being fine weather and a fair wind, we put to sea, and continued sailing with a pleasant breeze until the 7th, when we were met by a heavy gale of wind, which blew quite contrary for us; in consequence of that, we were obliged to put into the nearest port, which happened to be Torbay, where we came to an anchor, and remained there four days. During the little time that we had been on board, between twenty and thirty men were taken ill again with that ague and fever, who were put on shore at this port, as soon as the weather did permit. On the 12th, in the morning, the weather being a little calmer and the wind rather in our favour, a signal was made to put to sea again,

48

and steer for Lisbon, under the protection of a man of war brig. So having secured our anchors, we put to sea, and being but four ships in company, we made all sail that possibly we could. The wind continued blowing very hard for several days, by which we made great speed; and on the 27th, we hove in sight of Lisbon, and in the evening came to an anchor in the river Tagus, very convenient to Lisbon, and on the following morning, we disembarked in Black Horse Square.

This is a very large square, the buildings are stone, which appear to be very strong, and are about three stories high: the windows are ranged in a line, much the same as in this country, and open in the middle, (something like double doors), in order to pass out for air or for pleasure; for outside of the windows is a sort of iron railing, about three feet and a half high, and projects about two feet:—this is a common thing in Portugal and Spain. In the middle of the square stands a black horse, much resembling that in Queen's Square, in Bristol, only much larger, which formerly had a pair of diamond stones placed in the head, that resembled the eyes; but in the year 1808, when the French left Lisbon with the honours of war, by the consent of *Rimple*, they robbed this horse of his eyes; and not only robbed this horse of his eyes, but plundered every place they came to, particularly the chapels; for there was formerly a parcel of gold and silver images in the chapels, which the inhabitants did worship; but in nearly every town that the French marched through at that time, they took all that they could

49

find. Now being landed, we were put into Campoderick barracks, at Lisbon; and in about three or four days after our arrival there, I was promoted to the rank of a corporal.

We remained in Lisbon until the 10th of June, when, in consequence of troops being wanted up the country, we commenced our march for Thomar, taking our route through Santarem. Santarem is a large town which stands on a hill, and contains many large convents; but the streets are very dirty; indeed the streets in that country are seldom clean. On the 18th of June, we marched into Thomar, where we were put into a large convent that stood on a hill, nearly close to the town. This convent is large enough to hold twenty thousand men, occasionally; the walls are bomb-proof, but the town is not so large as Cirencester. In a few days after our arrival in this town the 1st Royals and 38th regiment of foot arrived, and took up their quarters in the convent with us. These two regiments and ours were immediately formed into a brigade, under the command of Lieutenant General Sir James Leith.

We remained at Thomar until September, when we received orders to proceed further up the country, for the enemy was advancing very rapidly: therefore, we commenced our march, and continued till we came to Buzacco, where we joined our army. We did not make a show of ourselves on the top of the hill that day, for the enemy was then about two miles distance, on the other side; so we took up our camp ground a little under the hill, and being rather short of provisions at

F

50

that time, and having a little money in my possession,
I purchased a small sheep, for which I gave four shillings and sixpence; and having three other men in my
mess, two killed and dressed the sheep, while the other
two were getting wood and water for the purpose of
cooking. The sheep, when dressed, weighed about
thirty pounds, which we cut up into small joints, on
the turf, as decently as we could; and being pretty
well assured that we should fall in with the enemy on
the morrow, we boiled the whole that night: so having
a little sea biscuit, we made a very hearty supper,
without any vegetables whatever. During our cookery,
our captain was frequently walking by us, but for what
reason we did not know: but however, it came into my
mind that he would like to partake of a little of our
mutton, but did not like to ask for it; therefore, we
agreed to send him a small joint, which he accepted
with a smile. The fragments that remained, we divided, each man taking his share; that if we should be
separated on the morrow, neither of us would be at a
loss for something to eat.

Having put every thing in readiness, for fear of any
alarm in the night, we laid ourselves down on the turf,
in order to get a little rest: it then being about ten
o'clock at night, the stars shone very bright, and every
thing seemed to be still, except the lizard, which
made the evening appear very pleasant. The lizard
continued running about very busy, frequently running
over us: some are very large, I suppose six or eight
inches round, and from the head to the point of the

51

tail, are twelve or fourteen inches in length; they are
not all so large, and are of many different colours; some
are very handsome, but so tame and so harmless, that
we seldom took any notice of their running over us:
we therefore took our repose very comfortably, until
about an hour before break of day, when we were
ordered to stand to our arms, which is a customary
thing when convenient to the enemy.

Before it was well day-light, we were alarmed by
a sharp firing of musketry, which proved to be with our
out-lying piquets and the enemy; in consequence of
which, we were immediately ordered to proceed to the
top of the heights, about one mile to our left. The
enemy made a grand attack on the right flank, but was
soon repulsed with great loss: they likewise made a very
bold attack on the left, for which place our brigade was
making all speed; but before we could reach our destination, the enemy had got possession: several columns
made their appearance on the top of the hill, and commenced firing on us, very sharply, before we were
hard'y within musket shot: we were then ordered to
load, but not to fire a shot till ordered. So we continued moving on in open column of companies, until
we got within about one hundred yards of them,
when we were ordered to wheel into line, and give
them a volley, which we immediately did, and saluted
them with three cheers and a charge, taking the signal
from General Leith, who commanded our brigade:—he
made the signal by taking off his hat and twirling it
over his head. The enemy stood their ground till we

F. 2.

52

got within twenty yards of them; but seeing that it was our intention to use the bayonet, they took to their heels, and made off as well as they could. We continued to fire, advancing down the hill as far as it was thought necessary, and being so close to their heels, there was great slaughter among them. So, the enemy being got near the bottom of the hill, and having a brigade of guns placed on a little hill just on the other side of the valley, cannon shot and shells began to fly among us very sharply; in consequence of that, the brigade was obliged to retreat to the top of the hill, leaving the light companies extended along about the middle of the hill, with an order to lie down behind any thing that would cover them, but not two to be together.

During this time, our brigade of guns came up, and was placed a little down the hill; and as soon as our line was out of their way, they commenced firing at the enemy's guns, which soon put them to the route. Very convenient to the enemy's guns, a column had formed up close to an ammunition waggon, and while in the act of taking ammunition out of the waggon, our gunners by chance placed a shell just in the middle of it; the moment it fell, it burst, by which the ammunition immediately blew up, carrying several men to a considerable height in the air, and likewise killed and wounded many that were standing round the waggon, which put the column into such confusion, that they began to run in all directions, leaving the wounded to shift for themselves.

53

They did not make any further attack that day; but towards the evening, they fell back about three miles: so we took up our camp ground on the top of the heights, on the same spot where a column of the enemy stood when we gave them the first volley. There the dead lay so thick, that we could not make it convenient to lie down in any comfort; therefore we set to work, and drew them a little distance away:—thirty-two were on that bit of ground that our company was to lie down on.

So having cleared our ground, we sat ourselves down in order to get a little refreshment, for our commissary had brought us a little rum: but nevertheless, I could not make myself so comfortable as I did the night before, for in this action, I was deprived of two of my messmates, who were wounded and taken to an hospital: but however, our loss on this occasion was very moderate, not having more than sixty of our regiment killed and wounded. After a little refreshment, we laid ourselves down without any expectation of getting any sleep, for we were not allowed to take off our accoutrements, for fear that the enemy should make an attack in the night; but however they did not: for soon after it was dark, they made a great quantity of fires from the right to the left of their line, which appeared to us most beautiful. The fires were kept good till about the middle of the night, when we supposed they were for taking a little rest; therefore we remained very quiet till about an hour before day-light, when we were ordered to stand to our arms, as usual, which we did; but before it was hardly break of day, we received orders to retreat towards Coimbra with all speed; for the enemy had been on their march for several hours, with an intention to out-flank us, with a much superior force. But however, their intention proved unsuccessful, for we took the nearest way across fields, &c. making all the speed that possibly we could, till we arrived on the other side of Coimbra, which was about eight leagues. A regiment of dragoons formed our rear guard, which was obliged to be very alert, being several times obliged to attack the enemy's advance, otherwise they would have been in Coimbra before us; for as we were going out of that town on the one side, the enemy was coming in on the other side. But when we were through the town, we had one thing in our favour, that was the Mondego river, which ran very deep and wide for several miles each way, and close to the town. Therefore, immediately after we were over the bridge, a brigade of guns was placed very near the bridge, in a direction to play over it and likewise to the gates of the town, which put a stop to their pursuit, there being no other way to come to the bridge, except through the gates; for the town is surrounded with a wall, but no other fortifications. Coimbra is the largest town in Portugal, except Lisbon, but the streets are not so clean nor so wide; and some of the buildings are four or five stories high. There are several large convents in the town, which were always made use of for hospitals, when in our possession.

55

We encamped near Coimbra two days, where we took refuge from the heavy dews of the night under the branches of the olive trees; for in that part of the country, there is a great quantity. The olive trees grow something like the plum or damson in England, only smaller in the leaf: the leaf is always green, and the berries very much resemble acorns, both in size and shape. The olive berries and the grape are the chief produce of the country: and it has been the case sometimes, that we have been obliged to encamp in the vineyards when the grapes have been in full bloom. The grape vine is very low; the main stock of the vine is not more than fourteen or sixteen inches high, which is pruned regularly once a year; they are planted in rows so near together, that the branches will run one among the other. We have also been encamped in an orange orchard. The orange trees run rather low, so that we could stand on the ground and gather the fruit off the lower branches. The orange trees are seldom without some fruit on them, for when one crop is nearly ripe, another will make its appearance. In some parts of the country there are a great many chesnuts, which are made use of about in the same manner as potatoes in England: they are good either boiled or roasted. There are but few potatoes rose in this country, at least I never saw any but what were brought from England or Ireland.

During these two days, the enemy were busy in making preparations to cross the river; so, in consequence of our army being so weak, we were obliged

to make all speed towards the heights of Soberal, at
which place there was a very strong fort that had previously been made by our engineers, and likewise a
line of batteries, in communication with that fort, which
extended across that part of the country from the
Tagus river, near Villa Franca, to the sea near Torres
Vedras. The grand fort is about seven leagues from
Lisbon. So we continued retreating till we came to
our destination, where we formed ourselves in line with
our batteries, some at camp where it was necessary, and
some at quarters. Our brigade took their route through
Pombal to Leyria, and from thence to Valverde, and
through Francos to Torres Vedras, (a town something
larger than Cirencester), where we took up our quarters.

On this retreat, the roads were crowded with the
the inhabitants, who were making their retreat towards
Lisbon, and loaded like bees with the principal part of
their property; for the enemy paid no respect to per-
sons, they plundered every thing they came near to.
So those who had got any valuable property in their
possession, made their retreat to Lisbon, leaving their
houses, furniture, and other effects, to the mercy of the
enemy. Now being at quarters at Torres Vedras, we
remained very comfortable and peaceable till after
Christmas; for the enemy never made an attack on our
brigade during the time we remained at that place;
but they made several attacks on different parts of our
line, but without success, for they were always repulsed
in a short time.

57

While we were at Torres Vedras, we were alarmed one night by a sudden shock of an earthquake; and it being about midnight, we were all very quiet taking our repose, but in consequence of so sudden a shock, we were all roused in an instant. It appeared something like being rocked in a cradle, but it did not continue more than half a minute. But our company being in a house by ourselves, and no other inhabitants, we could not be certain what was the matter: some ran out into the street as quick as possible, without any thing on but their shirts, exclaiming, " The house " will be down !" but no sooner were they out in the street, than they were accompanied by some other companies in about the same condition. Some inhabitants being very convenient, and hearing the soldiers in such confusion, looked out at their windows and told us what was the matter: they did not seem much alarmed, for they said they had several times found of an earthquake before. We then retired to rest as before, something better reconciled.

In the beginning of January, our brigade received orders to proceed to the heights of Soberal, which we did, and took up our camp ground very convenient to the grand fort. The enemy had possession of Soberal, which was about two miles distance from the grand fort, but they did not make any attack on that part of the line, only with the out-lying piquets; them they would frequently be teazing with a few musket shot. So now being exposed to all weathers at that time of the year, we were allowed double tents.

The while we remained here, our army was still increasing; our regiment was joined by a detatchment of one hundred and fifty men, some from the second battalion, and some that had been left behind in England with the ague; and most regiments about the same, either more or less, and likewise small parties frequently joined from Lisbon hospitals. At this place we got our provisions very regularly, sometimes salt provisions, and sometimes fresh: we had also a little rum most days, which was served out in the morning before day-light; for at such times as these, or as I might say, at all times when convenient to the enemy, we stood to our arms one hour before break of day, and remained till it was broad day-light, in order to be ready should the enemy make any movement.

We continued at camp till March, when the enemy began to retreat towards the borders of Spain; for not having sufficient food, that occasioned their retreat: therefore, we made a very rapid advance after them, through Santarem to Pumbal: very convenient to that town our light division fell in with them about the middle of the day. No general action took place, but a continued skirmishing along the road till night. In Pumbal there is one large convent, which the enemy left in a miserable looking condition; most of the boarded floors were pulled up for the purpose of making fires, and all the doors beat to pieces. Between Pumbal and Condesh, which is about four leagues, the enemy threw large trees across the road, in several places, in order to check our guns; but however, that

59

was not of much consequence, for we always had plenty
of tools of all descriptions, in case of necessity.

When we came within sight of Condesh, we beheld several parts of the town in a blaze of fire: this
the enemy had done as a sort of spite to the inhabitants,
because they could find no provisions in the town. They
also destroyed every thing they came near, and not only
in that town, but in many others; and if they found any
corn, and could not take it away, they would strew it
about the road in the dirtiest place they could find, or
throw it into a river if there was one convenient: and
what wine they could not make use of, they let run out
of the barrels. The barrels are in general very large,
and it being rather too much trouble to beat them to
pieces, they would put several musket balls through
them, which made them useless. Condesh is two leagues
from Coimbra, on the main road, and about as large as
Lechlade.

But the whole of the enemy's army did not retreat
through Coimbra; some took a cross-country road to
Pontamasela, (which is about five leagues to the right
of Coimbra), and we continued advancing in pursuit of
them with all possible speed; in consequence of that,
when they came to within about one league of that
place, they were obliged to leave some of their officers'
baggage behind, and a parcel of neddy-asses, which
they had for the purpose of carrying baggage: but, because they should be of no use to us, the barbarous
wretches ham-stringed them: had they shot them, the
poor animals would have been out of their misery. But

however, they soon paid dear enough for that; for in order to check our advance, they destroyed the bridge, by way of blowing it up with powder; but in consequence of some neglect of their engineers, the bridge blew up before they could get their rear guard over, so by that, our advance, which was the light brigade, gave them three cheers and a charge, which caused some to surrender themselves prisoners of war, and some to take to the river, by which about four hundred of them were drowned; for at that place, the current ran very strong and deep.

Night coming on, we took up our camp ground in a wood on this side of the river for that night, and part of the next day, the while our reconnoitrers were plumbing the river for a shallow place to get over. At this time we were very short of provisions, not having more than two ounces of rice, each man, for three days, besides our meat, for we in general got some meat, or as I might say, what was called meat; but sometimes it was not worthy of that name, for we always drove the bullocks with us, and if we had a few good ones when we started, the best were always kept till last; and when on the march, they seldom ever get any thing to eat, except what they get themselves on the road side as they go along; for at night, they are put into some place or other where, most likely, there is nothing for them to eat; so that they continue getting worse and worse: therefore, we seldom ever got a bit of good meat, after being a few days on the march.

61

However, as some of our company were walking about a small village very convenient to the camp, they found a great quantity of Indian corn, which they happily loaded themselves with, together with some eating oil that they by chance found in another house; for the whole of the inhabitants had evacuated the village: but in consequence of our making such a rapid advance, the enemy had not time to plunder this village. Therefore, being very hungry, and having some of this Indian corn, we set to work with our camp-kettle lids, (which we in general used for frying pans), and fried some of it with the oil—it was something like eating parched peas: but however, most of us made a hearty meal, for hunger is very bad.

This Indian corn is raised in many places in Portugal, and mostly planted where the ground lies low and moist; it grows with a stalk as large as broad bean stalks, and about as high; the ear is in general about six inches long and about four inches round, the corn is very yellow and as large as gray peas, and the poor people seldom ever eat any bread but what is made of it. This bread is very good when hot and just taken out of the oven, but when stale, it is very middling eating.

I think it worth notice to say, that there was one thing much unpleasanter eating than Indian corn, and which was commonly made use of on this advance, that was bullock's blood: for every day, as soon as our butchers arrived with the bullocks, the men would flock round them with their mess kettles, like a swarm

G

of bees, in comparison, and the moment that a bullock was stuck, there was such pushing and thronging, to catch the blood, almost as if it was good wine, and frequently some dispute would take place in the scuffle; and I have actually seen many blows passed in consequence of the same. To prevent such disputes, the butchers made a charge of one shilling for the blood of one bullock; but at length, when this news reached the ears of our general officers, means were immediately taken to prevent it altogether.

About the middle of the day, orders came to stand to our arms and proceed to the Mondego river; and when we came there, it was a heartless place to behold. A sheet of water, about fifty yards wide, and in some places nearly three feet deep. Many of our women were obliged to wade through the river, which I was heartily sorry to see; but it was not in my power, nor any other man's, to give them any assistance. But, however, all got safe over, except two or three neddy-asses, which, in consequence of being so heavy loaded, were carried away with the force of the current.

When all were over, we continued our advance as before, and crossed three other small rivers the following day, but we did not overtake the enemy any more till we came to Guarda, which was about seventy miles; and about three miles from that town, our light division fell in with their rear guard, when a sharp skirmishing took place; but night coming on, it did not continue long: therefore we took up our camp ground very convenient to Guarda for that night. Guarda is a large

63

town which stands on a mountain, and I have been informed, it is the highest inhabited mountain in Europe; but the truth I cannot ascertain.

The enemy continued retreating great part of that night; and on the following morning, we advanced in the usual manner, but did not fall in with them for several days. But in consequence of their having possession of Almeida, they formed a line on the plains of Villa Formosa. Our sixth division invested Almeida, and remained to attack a division of the enemy that was coming to relieve the garrison, and the remaining part of our army formed a line very convenient to the enemy's line, which was about three leagues from Almeida.

On the 5th of May, the enemy made a false attack on the left, and a grand attack on the right, but was received most gallantly, and repulsed with great loss both of infantry and cavalry. Our loss on this occasion, I cannot ascertain; but several regiments suffered very much. On the following morning, the enemy fired sixteen guns, as a signal to Almeida, that there was no relief for them: therefore they retreated again; some took refuge in Ciudad Rodrigo, (which is a garrison town), and the remaining part fell back to Salamanca. So, by that, our army fell back a little distance into Portugal, and took up our cantonments in the different villages that were most convenient, leaving our second brigade by Almeida, which consisted of the 4th, the 30th, and 44th regiments of foot.

G 2

64

The same night, they who were in Almeida finding there was no relief for them, spiked the guns that were round the garrison, and blew up the magazines, about the middle of the night, and left the town. But where our second brigade was, the while the enemy were making their escape, I cannot ascertain; but however, as soon as they were apprized of the enemy's movement, they proceeded on their march in pursuit of them with all speed, towards St. Felice, in Spain. Our brigade not being far off, we soon got intelligence, and in consequence of that, the light companies of the brigade were immediately dispatched off in pursuit of them, with all possible speed, without knapsacks; and on the following morning, about ten o'clock, we fell in with them on the road near Barbadepork, when a sharp skirmishing took place, which was not finally settled for nearly five hours. At length, it was thought necessary to show them the point of the bayonet and give them a charge, which we did with great vigour; for having no knapsacks, we could out-run the enemy, as they were loaded with the plunder of Almeida. The enemy seeing what was our intention, they turned their backs to us and ran as fast as possibly they could; and in a few minutes they came to the brink of a hill, a place that they were not very well acquainted with, for in one place was a very steep rugged rock, between twenty and thirty yards in length, and a considerable distance to the bottom; and in consequence of their retreating so rapidly, many of them were not able to make a stop so sudden, but went headlong down the rock, by which some met with present death, and some with broken arms and legs.

Our line was within a few yards of the enemy when they began to descend this hill, but seing so many disappear in a moment, that gave us a little warning, and upon that we shortened our pace, at the same time the bugle sounded to halt and commence firing, which we did just on the brink of the hill, and continued firing till the enemy were quite out of the reach of musket shot. At the bottom of this hill was a river, that ran very strong, and in some places very deep, by which several were drowned in crossing; so we did not make any attempt to advance any further. Of course, our duty did not call us any further, for on the other side of the river was another very long hill, and no doubt but the enemy would have been glad to have catched us on the other side of the river; but however, British soldiers are not so easily led into an error : we therefore kept our ground on the brink of the hill, and the enemy retreated about one mile beyond the river towards St. Felice, being then about two miles from that town.

About seven o'clock in the evening, the enemy sent a flag of truce, requesting to be favoured with the liberty to come and pick up their wounded, which was immediately granted, and likewise ten men from each light company to assist them. Their loss on this occasion was very great, and most melancholy to behold.

The while this was being executed, and our own wounded being secured, night began to approach us, so upon that, the three light companies that belonged to the first brigade (which was ours) received orders to retreat back to their different regiments that night; for we had nothing to eat all that day, neither was there any thing to be got until we could reach our quarters, which were about four leagues distant: therefore we commenced our march about nine o'clock at night, with middling good spirits, and joined our regiment between one and two o'clock on the following morning; but before we could hardly reach our quarters, we got very tired, and, I might venture to say, almost exhausted for want of food and rest. Our second brigade having a little provisions with them, they remained on their ground till next morning, and buried the dead. In a few days after this, our division fell back about fifty miles further into Portugal, and took up their cantonments in the different villages, about ten leagues from Coimbra:—our regiment took up their quarters in Travanca.

On this short march I was taken very ill with the fever, as were many others, and in consequence of that, a general order was given for the whole of the sick to be sent to Coimbra; therefore, each man was provided with a mule which carried us to that town: but when we came there, we found ourselves worse off still, for in consequence of the hospitals being so crowded with the wounded, we could not be taken in; therefore

we were obliged to content ourselves with room to lie
down in a passage of one of the hospitals till next morning, when we received orders to go to Lisbon by water.
So then some Portuguese boats were immediately got
ready, and we proceeded from thence down the Mondego river to Figuera, accompanied by a medical
officer; there we were put into an old house that had
not been inhabited for several years, and remained there
four days, when a ship was ready to sail which was
bound for Lisbon.

During this time, by not having proper assistance,
and the fatigue of the journey, most of us were getting
in a very weak state, so that we could hardly help ourselves. But however, being put on board, and a fair
wind, the ship was immediately put to sea, and on the
second day came to an anchor in the Tagus river. On
the following morning, we disembarked at Lisbon, and
were put into a hospital, where we got every assistance
that was needful. But nevertheless, there was one
thing that I did not very well approve of, that was the
way of burying the dead: for as soon as a man was
dead, he was sewed up in an old blanket, or in a piece
of calico, and put into a coffin and conveyed to the
burial ground on a car; but as soon as they arrived at
the grave, the coffin was placed just on one side of the
grave, turned over, and so let the corpse roll out into
the grave; a little mould was then thrown over, so that
it might not be seen, as the graves were, in general,
made large enough to take twenty or thirty bodies: the
corpse being covered over, the coffin was taken back to

the hospital, in order to be ready for another; so that one coffin would serve a hundred men as well as one.

In about six weeks, I recovered so as to be able to join the detachments at Belem barracks, which is about four miles from Lisbon; but some part of Belem joins Lisbon after the same manner as Chelsea joins London. I remained at these barracks about one month, by which time I was nearly recovered to my former state of health; for we were marched down to the sea regularly twice a week, in order to bathe for the benefit of our health. So now a party being wanted to go up to the army in charge of the regiment's clothing, I volunteered my service to go, as we were to go by water to Coimbra; for I thought that much better than marching, after being so lately ill. Therefore, our clothing being already on board a transport ship, we embarked ourselves, in company with parties of several other regiments that had clothing on board; and having every arrangement made that was necessary, we put to sea with a gentle breeze.

The weather continued calm and pleasant until the second day, when we arrived in Mondego Bay, and about sun-set, just as we were in the act of clearing away in order to drop our anchor, a most tremendous gale of wind sprung up, (which fortunately blew off the land), and in consequence of the bay being so rough, we were obliged to put to sea again and strike our topgallant-masts as quick as possible. So having done that, we hoisted the mainsail to the wind, and committed ourselves to the mercy of the Almighty.

69

This gale continued two days and nights, by which time we got within sight of the rock of Gibraltar, being then two hundred miles further from our destination than we were when at Lisbon. So the gale having ceased, and the wind blowing very steady, rather in our favour, we hoisted up our top-gallant-masts again and crowded as much sail as the weather would permit. The third day, we hove in sight of Lisbon, the place that we started from first; the weather was then very pleasant.

Notwithstanding, we had not passed all danger; for on the following night, after passing by Lisbon on our voyage as before, when all were between decks taking their repose, (except a few sailors that were on watch, who ought to have been awake), we were suddenly alarmed, about midnight, by a transport brig, which ran right across our ship. Hearing so sudden a crash, we thought we were foul of a rock, on which we began to run up on deck as quick as possible, and hearing some women that were on board squeak and squall in such a manner, we were all in great confusion for several minutes: but when we found what was the matter, and there being but little wind, we were soon reconciled. But it was nearly half an hour before we could be separated, and had there been a strong wind, one or both must certainly have gone to the bottom. Our rigging was very much damaged, and the main-sail torn all in ribbons: but fortunately, as our ship was much larger than the other, that was the principal damage that we received.

70

In a few minutes after we were clear off, the captain of the brig hailed us to lay to, and accompany him till morning; for the brig had received so much damage in her bows, that he was afraid he should not be able to reach Lisbon, which was not more than thirty miles. But however, soon after day-light, the captain hailed us again, and told us, that although the brig was in such a dangerous state, he would endeavour to make Lisbon harbour: so having repaired the principal part of our rigging, we made sail as before. But what could we suppose the sailors were about when this damage happened?—Why, they must have been all asleep, or not looking out as they ought to have been, for the moon shone very bright, so that a ship might have been seen at half a mile distance.

We continued sailing till the following morning, when we arrived in Mondego bay once more, and came to anchor as convenient to the shore as possible, and the next day we disembarked our stores at Figuera, where we remained several days, until some Portuguese boats were ready to take our stores; and then we proceeded up the Mondego river to Coimbra, (which is about nine or ten leagues), and from thence to the regiment at Travanca. They had been there very comfortable the whole time that I had been away, having nothing but their own regimental duty to do; and also good provisions and very regular. But in a short time after I joined the regiment, we received orders from Lord Wellington for a party of different trades, such as masons, carpenters, and miners, to go on a working party to Ciudad

Rodrigo, together with a party of engineers, as there
was a number from each regiment in the army to go and
assist the engineers in making batteries and breast-
works against that town: for of course we were obliged
to clear the country as we did go

Two divisions were very convenient during the
time that our works were being made, which had always a very strong picquet in readiness, should the
enemy sally out on our working party. So, when the
works were nearly completed, the remaining part of
the army received orders to proceed to that place. Our
division had about one hundred miles to march.

On this march we made regular stages, and took
up our quarters in the different towns and villages every
night, taking our route through Guarda, and on the
19th of January, 1812, we arrived at a village within
three leagues of our destination, and took up our quarters in the usual manner, with the intention to remain
there till next morning, and then to proceed to Ciudad
Rodrigo. But about eight o'clock in the evening, just
as we were thinking about taking a little rest, a dragoon came galloping into the village, with an order for
us to proceed to Ciudad Rodrigo without any delay
whatever; therefore we assembled as quick as possible
and made all speed for that place.

As our works had been completed two or three days
previous to this, and two divisions already there, a heavy
cannonading had been carried on, by which a breach
was sufficiently made; and about ten o'clock that night,
being the 19th of January, 1812, they who were there

began the glorious attack; and before we could arrive
to give any assistance, our army had got possession of
the garrison, but not without the loss of a great many
brave British soldiers, whose wives and relations had
to lament their melancholy fate. The garrison was attacked in three different places. The division that
entered the breach suffered greatly, being obliged to
fall back the second time; and likewise another division
suffered by being blown up with powder; for in one
place, the enemy had undermined the ramparts, and
laid a train for that purpose; but, fortunately, the explosion took place before one quarter of the division had
ascended the walls, otherwise there would have been
great slaughter.

When our division arrived, not having had a share
in the grand attack, we were put into possession of the
garrison, and the remaining part of the army went to
their different cantonments, as before. When we entered the garrison, it was a most miserable place to
behold; for the enemy's dead were lying about in all
directions, and the buildings beat to pieces by our cannon shot in a frightful manner, and several houses were
then on fire; in consequence of which, we were immediately set to work to extinguish the fire, and fortunately, by great exertion, we got the upper hand of it in a
short time. The next thing that was thought most
necessary for us to do, was to put the dead bodies
under ground and clear the streets, that the market
people might be able to come in with their goods as
soon as possible: for at that time there was not a thing

of any description to be got in the town, except a few
bags of French biscuits, and those our commissary
seized: therefore we were very busily employed the
first day, and not only the first, but every day, except
Sunday; for we were all hands put to work as soon as
possible, repairing the walls and ramparts round the
garrison, for fear the enemy should advance and attack
us in the ruins; but however, that did not happen to
be the case.

We remained there till the beginning of March, by
which time we had done the worst of the work; and in
consequence of there being another grand attack to be
made in another part of the country, a division of Spaniards was put in possession of this garrison, and our
division received orders to proceed to Badajos, in Spain,
which was about two hundred miles from this place:
but in consequence of the garrison being not quite
put in repair, we left a small party of our engineers to
finish it.

On this march, we made regular stages, and took
up our quarters in the different towns and villages
every night, taking our route, the first day to Aurela,
next to Calagas, and so on to St. Vincent, and then to
Castle Branco, (which is a large town), and from thence
to Villa Velha, and crossed the river Tagus. Near that
place, a floating bridge was made by our engineers, for
there was no established bridge near that place. From
thence to Niza, and halted there two nights; and from
there to Portalegre, which is a large town; from there
to Arronches, and next to Campo Major, which is a

H

small garrison town just on the borders of Portugal, five leagues from Badajos in Spain. Badajos is a large garrison town, which the enemy had got possession of, being a very strong fortified place: there is likewise a strong castle in the town, where the enemy intended to fly for refuge, should they be overpowered in other parts of the town.

We remained at Campo Major seven days, when it was supposed that our works at Badajos were nearly completed; for our engineers and three other divisions had been there some time, making batteries and breast-works against that town.

At Campo Major we could see Badajos very plain, although at five leagues distance; but sometimes the town was almost hid in a cloud of smoke that ascended from the enemy's guns, for they kept up almost a continual fire, with shot and shells, on our working parties from morning till night, by which many were killed and wounded; and likewise, a great quantity of our works was destroyed, some days, more than we could put together in a whole night. They would also throw a few random shells every night; but it being dark, as they could not see us, there were but few that did any damage; for a shell can always be seen very plain in the night, so that a party of men might be some little aware, if it did not explode before it fell. When a shell falls very near to a party of men, their plan is to fall down on their faces as quick as possible, and remain till the shell has exploded, by which means it has often been the case, that every man has escaped; but if the men should continue standing till the shell did explode, it is most likely that several would be killed or wounded: for a shell always flies upwards, and spreads very wide. These shells are filled with several sorts of combustibles, also with bits of iron, old nails, musket shot, &c.

Having an order to proceed to Badajos, we marched from Campo Major to Elvas, (which is another garrison town in Portugal), and from thence to the river Guadiana, where was another floating bridge that was made by our engineers. There we crossed the river and marched to Olivenza, and from thence to within one league of Badajos, where we took up our camp ground and remained several days: for in consequence of this garrison being so strongly fortified, our works could not be executed so soon as at Ciudad Rodrigo. But however, as soon as our works were completed, we commenced a very heavy fire with shot and shells, by which a breach was made in a short time, large enough to march in by subdivisions, and some part of the town was in a blaze of fire.

On the 6th of April, 1812, about ten o'clock at night, we began the glorious attack in four different directions, and all at one time as near as possible. The light division took the breach, much to their misfortune; for when they got within about one hundred yards of the breach, the enemy threw out some sort of fire-balls, which gave such a light round that part of the town, that they could see the division coming almost as plain as if it had been day-light, which was a great disadvantage to them, for the greatest part of the enemy had placed

76

themselves very convenient to the breach; in consequence of which, that division was repulsed three times. But the enemy finding they had something to do in other parts of the town, that gave the light division some little better chance: however, just as our division was going to ascend the ladder, unfortunately the cock of one of the men's muskets caught in one of the rounds of the ladder and went off, by which we were discovered before a man could make his landing good on the top of the walls, and a strong party of the enemy was there in two or three minutes, and began to pour down upon us in all directions, by which Major Gen. Walker, who commanded our second brigade, received four wounds in quick time. Previous to this, the enemy had placed large pieces of timber, stones, &c. just on the top of the walls all round the garrison, that as soon as we came under them, were to be rolled off down on our heads; and in consequence of which many were severely wounded.

But while the enemy were so busily employed at this and two other places, the third division, which was commanded by General Picton, got possession of the castle. The enemy did not expect that we should attempt to make any attack in that place, for the ditches were very deep and the walls a most extensive height. The walls were considerably higher than we expected, for when the division came under them, their ladders were not long enough by a great deal, by which they found great difficulty in ascending: but however, as they had no opposition, they did get up by some means

77

or other; and as soon as three or four hundred had got possession, they gave three cheers as loud as possible they could, which very much alarmed the enemy, and put them in great confusion. Upon that, the whole began to make for the castle, not thinking that we had got possession; and in a few minutes, when we had assembled a party together, we followed after with all speed, as did also the other divisions in like manner. But when the enemy came to the castle, to their great surprise and mortification, they were not permitted to enter. So having lost their principal object, they soon threw down their arms, and surrendered themselves prisoners of war: therefore, about four o'clock in the morning, the whole garrison was in our possession, and about two thousand prisoners besides their wounded.

Our loss on this occasion was very great and most melancholy to behold: the light division, that entered at the breach, were the greatest sufferers; and to see so many brave British soldiers lying dead, one across the other, it occasioned many a man to shed tears, in particular when we saw two women lamenting over their dead husbands.

Having secured the prisoners, the next thing was to secure our wounded comrades, and then to bury the dead, which was done without delay. In this garrison was an immense quantity of provisions; we likewise found a large vault under ground, nearly full of French brandy, which contained several thousand gallons, in

H 3

which place a drummer of our regiment and two or three men of other regiments were drowned.

On the following day, having put our wounded into hospitals, and every arrangement made that was necessary, we marched out to our camp as before, and a division of Spaniards was put in possession of the garrison, together with a party of our engineers, who were left to put the garrison in repair. So we remained at our camp four days, and then commenced our march up the country again, taking nearly the same route as we came down, till we came to Aurela, when we took a cross-country road, further into the centre of Portugal, leaving Guarda on our right. Our division took up their quarters within a few miles of Viseu, which is a large town, in which there are several large convents. So we remained in our cantonments very comfortable, about one month, where we got good provisions and very regular, and nothing in particular to do but our regimental duty, till we received orders to proceed towards Salamanca, in Spain, which was about thirty leagues.

On this march, we made regular stages till we arrived within a few leagues of Salamanca, and took up our quarters in the different towns and villages every night; taking our route through Viseu to Transcosa, next to Pinhel, and so on to St. Felices, which was the first town that we came to in Spain: and from thence to Villa Veira, and through several other villages, till we arrived within about two leagues of Salamanca.

Here we formed our camp, very convenient to the river Tormes, till the following morning, when we were obliged to ford the river; for about one thousand of the enemy had garrisoned themselves in a large convent, just on the outside of the town, which commanded the bridge; but their main body had retreated, and formed line about two leagues beyond Salamanca: therefore, we passed by the town, and formed opposite the enemy's line, about one league from Salamanca, (where we could see them very plain), leaving our fourth division to attack the convent.

Round this convent were three lines of walls, one within the other, which were very high; the inside wall was much higher than those on the outside; the convent was very large, and three stories high, with several pieces of cannon on each story, in order to fire out at the windows. The enemy had been between two and three years rebuilding and fortifying this convent, which was taken by one division of our army in nine days.

Not being very well aware of this place, a false attempt was made to storm the second day, in order to find out their principal fortifications, for they had not shown the guns that were at the windows till then; but they did not forget to show them as soon as we came near enough: but however, we did not remain in their reach long enough to feel much of the effects of them then, for it was thought almost impossible to take it by storm, without the loss of a considerable number of men: and as Lord Wellington had some knowledge of this fortification before we advanced out of Portugal, he thought it necessary to take a brigade of battering train with the army to this place; and as there were no other means of getting possession, but by battering it down or by setting fire to it, a battery was formed as quick as possible, and commenced firing at the corner of one wing of the convent, as near the foundation as possible, in order to beat it down. So a continual firing was kept up, till the wall at that end was battered all to pieces, three or four feet above the ground; but as the building was so tied with timber, it continued standing; so by that, it was thought proper to try what a few red-hot shot would do. Therefore a furnace was erected for that purpose without delay; and on the —th of July, 1812, about eleven o'clock in the forenoon, we began to throw red-hot shot into the upper part of that wing of the convent that was so battered at the bottom; in consequence of which, several places were soon in a blaze of fire. At the same time, our battering train kept up a continual fire at the convent in all directions; but the enemy kept their stations in spite of all, even in that wing that was on fire, where they could, till at length, all of a sudden, the whole wing came down to the ground, which buried nearly two hundred of the unfortunate wretches in the ruins: this put the remaining part into great confusion. So immediately after it fell, when all was in a blaze and in such confusion, we made a bold attack, and soon got possession of the walls without any great opposition: therefore, before four o'clock in the afternoon, the convent was in our

81

possession, and about seven hundred prisoners, a great
quantity of ammunition, and sixty pieces of cannon,
besides what were in use. There was also a great
quantity of working tools of all descriptions, which appeared to have been manufactured in that place; for
several branches of trade were carried on in the convent, and it seemed to appear that they continued busy
at their work till almost the minute that we began the
attack; for when we entered the convent, they had
good fires at their forges, and their tools lying about on
their work as if just thrown down to go to dinner.

Our loss on this occasion was but trifling: therefore having secured the prisoners and extinguished the
fire, we left this fortification to the direction of the governor of Salamanca, to do with it as he thought proper.

Previous to the convent being taken, the main
army and that party that was in the convent would
make signals to each other every night, by way of
throwing up some sort of rockets. Their army made
several signals the same night after the convent was
taken; but to their great surprise, they could get no
answer, which I suppose was rather mortifying to
them: therefore on the following morning, about one
hour before day-light, they began to retreat further
into Spain, and at day-light we advanced in pursuit of
them, taking nearly the same route as they did, till we
came to Navadelrea, where we were obliged to halt
and take a little rest; for the enemy had extended
themselves along the other side of the river Douro, about

two leagues beyond Navadelrea, with a great body of men, and some heavy cannon at each pass.

So we formed our line, about one league from the enemy, between Navadelrea and the Douro; but in consequence of the weather being so extremely hot at that time, we marched into Navadelrea during the heat of the day, each brigade leaving a strong piquet to watch the enemy's manœuvres; and at sun-set in the evening, we marched out to camp, in order to be ready should the enemy make any movement. Some part of the night we were allowed to wrap ourselves up in our blankets and lie down, but not to take off our accoutrements on any pretence whatever; and should we be allowed to lie still four or five hours, (as by chance we were sometimes), our blankets would be almost as wet outside, merely with the dews of the night, as if it had been a storm of rain; for in that country, and likewise in Portugal, the dews of the night are in general very heavy; and I think, the warmer the weather, the heavier the dews.——From Salamanca to this place was a very fruitful and pleasant country.

However, in consequence of the enemy having a strong reinforcement of troops from France, and there being no possibility of our crossing the river, we did not remain there more than nine days; for it was thought necessary to fall back a little, so as to entice the enemy to follow us till we could get to some place where we should have a little more advantage than at this place to engage them. Therefore, as soon as we began to fall back, which was a little before break of day, on the 18th of July, the enemy immediately advanced after us, as close to our heels as possible. But nothing in particular happened the first day; but the second day was a busy day with our cavalry, for they were skirmishing with the enemy's advance great part of the day: nevertheless, we formed our camp in the evening, as convenient to wood and water as possible, in the usual manner, near Hornillos, but not without throwing out strong piquets to watch the enemy's movements, should there be any. Therefore, after a little refreshment, we laid ourselves down, but without any hopes of getting much rest, for we were not allowed to unroll our blankets, neither to take off our accoutrements.

We lay still ti'l about midnight, when we stood to our arms, and marched about three miles towards the enemy on the plains, and there we remained under arms till day-light, when we found ourselves close to the enemy's piquets. Our army was formed in three lines, and our guns were placed between in the intervals, and every thing in readiness to engage. Soon after day-light the enemy began to manœuvre and form columns in different directions; but it being on the plains, where they could find no possibility of taking any advantage, they would not come on. Our cavalry advanced two or three times and gave them a few shots, in order to bring them to, but we could not entice them to come on by any means whatever, neither did any action take place that day; for about nine or ten o'clock in the forenoon, we could observe the enemy filing off round

our right flank, in order to get to Salamanca, if there
was a possibility, before us; in consequence of which,
we were obliged to continue our retreat a little further.

The enemy took to the mountains which led towards Salamanca, and our army took the valleys, across
hedge and ditch, fields of corn, vineyards, &c. just
alongside of the enemy; some times so near together,
that they would give us a few cannon shot off the
mountains. Our cavalry took their route between the
two armies, by which a little skirmishing took place
with them and the enemy's cavalry several times in the
day, but nothing further.

We continued retreating in this manner till the
evening of the following day, when we arrived within
about two leagues of Salamanca: the enemy were still
in possession of the hills, but nevertheless, our army
was formed as close to them as possible, in order to
stop their advancing any further, unless we should be
overpowered.

This evening, the commander in chief of the French
army sent a message to the governor of Salamanca, requesting him to make preparations for the staff of his
army, for they should enter the town at such an hour
next morning; this put the inhabitants rather in confusion,
for in that town the French and Spaniards could not
agree so well as in some other parts of Spain. But notwithstanding all this, Lord Wellington was determined
to put a stop to their pursuit, if there was a possibility;
therefore our out-lying piquets were placed as near the
enemy as possible: and fortunately, this evening we had

85

two or three fine regiments of infantry joined to the army, which had lately arrived from England, and also a fine regiment of German dragoons; so about ten o'clock at night, we piled our arms and sat down, but we were not permitted to take off even our knapsacks, for fear the enemy should make a sudden advance in the night.

This night proved to us a very uncomfortable one; for we had not been sitting many minutes, when a most tremendous storm of thunder and lightning came on, attended with such heavy rain as is very seldom known. Having neither house nor harbour to fly to for shelter, you may suppose that our situation was very unpleasant; and in consequence of two or three claps of thunder being so tremendously loud, our dragoon horses were so startled, that many broke loose from where they were tied, and began to run in all directions, by which several could not be found any more—it was supposed they ran into the enemy's lines, and it is most likely they did.

The weather continued very heavy for a little more than half an hour, when it began to abate; and about midnight it got quite calm, and the stars shone very bright and pleasant, by which we passed the remaining part of the night in a little more comfort, although our clothing was very wet.

About one hour before break of day, we stood to our arms in the usual manner, and soon after day-light appeared, being the 22d of July, 1812, a sharp skirmishing took place with our out-lying picquets and the enemy. Our cavalry were immediately ordered to ad-

I

vance, which they did, and continued skirmishing for two or three hours, for the main body did not come on so rapidly as we expected; but seeing our army formed already for combat, they began manœuvring and changing their position; in consequence of which, we were obliged to change our position; and about nine o'clock, the action became general.

Though their thundering cannon roared tremendously, yet Lord Wellington was determined on victory; therefore we did not fail to let them hear the thunder of our cannon; and as our regiment formed part of the first line, we did not forget to let them hear and feel the effects of our small arms, and according to English custom, as soon as we could make it convenient, we showed them the point of the bayonet, and gave them a grand charge, by which we obliged them to leave three pieces of cannon in our possession in a short time: this part of of the enemy's line continued retreating for some considerable distance, and we continued firing advancing, till it was thought necessary for us to halt, which accordingly we did, and remained on our ground for some time, expecting they would advance again; but however, they did not advance on that part of the line any more, so that our division came off rather favourably: but in some other parts of the line the action continued till it was quite dark night.

A large column of the enemy had placed themselves on a very steep high hill, where it seemed they were determined to keep possession; for the fourth division of our army made an attack on that hill three

times and was repulsed every time: but however, Lord
Wellington was determined to have the hill if there
was a possibility; therefore the fourth attack was made
when nearly dark, so that they could hardly see each
other, with a determination not to be conquered as long
as a man was standing; in consequence of which there
was great slaughter on both sides for several minutes,
but at length, when the enemy found what was our
intention, they soon gave way, and a great number
threw down their arms and surrendered themselves
prisoners: and as soon as they had lost the hill, their
whole army retreated about one league, but we remained on our ground that night, and sent out our
picquets as usual towards the enemy, and a little after
ten o'clock there was silence on both sides. So then
the first thing that was most necessary for us to do, was
to search for the wounded; but in consequence of it
being dark, and among bushes, &c. many lay bleeding
in their gore till next morning.

It plainly appeared to us this day, that the enemy
were supplied with a load of provisions for a long advance, just as if they were certain of driving us back
into Portugal again; for in several places where they
had been so closely pursued by our army, they left a
great quantity behind, which fell into our hands: however, in the course of this day most of us got loaded
with what they left behind; for some found small bags
of biscuit, about ten or twelve pounds weight; some,
small bags of flour, about the same weight; and some,
joints of mutton and goat's flesh; all of which we found

I 2

very acceptable, for at that time we were rather short of provisions.

So when our camp was formed, and our picquets posted, the remaining part were soon very busily employed in providing for the belly: some making hard dumplings with the flour that we had found, some getting wood, and others searching for water for our cooking, which by chance was found at about one mile distance from our camp. Therefore towards the middle of the night, we enjoyed ourselves over a most noble supper, and after a little conversation over what had passed during the day, we wrapped ourselves up in our blankets, with our accoutrements on, and lay down in hopes of getting a few hours' good rest, for we were then getting very much fatigued for want of sleep.

However we did not get much sleep that night, for between two and three o'clock in the morning we were alarmed by the sound of the enemy's trumpets, at which time they began to retreat further into Spain again, towards Valladolid; and before four o'clock in the morning, our army began to advance in pursuit of them with all speed, leaving the dead on the ground for the inhabitants to bury: but it is most likely they were not put under ground, for it was generally the case that the Spaniards would burn every dead body that they found lying on the ground, (and certainly there was a great number killed in this action), but whether that was the case at this place or not, I cannot ascertain.

Having a regiment of German dragoons, that had just arrived from England, as before mentioned,

89

with such strong and powerful horses, they formed our advance guard, and about the middle of the day they fell in with a party of the enemy, consisting of about sixteen hundred, which formed their rear guard, and when they found our dragoons advancing so rapidly, they formed themselves into solid square, and so retreated a little distance in that manner, in hopes of making their escape. But however, the Germans did not stand manœuvring with them long, for they put spurs to their horses, and charged them with such vigour, that their square was broken in a few minutes; in consequence of which the enemy threw down their arms on the spot and surrendered themselves prisoners of war, for they could plainly see there was no possibility of making their escape.

In the first town we marched through, which was about five leagues from Salamanca, was a large convent, in which place the enemy had placed about one thousand men that had been wounded in the action the day before, and so conveyed to this place; but in consequence of being so closely pursued by our army, they were not able to convey them any further; so they were left in this place without any surgeon or any attendance whatever, supposing that we should find them attendance. But however, Lord Wellington was not to be trifled with in that manner, for our surgeons had enough to do to attend to our own wounded, and to them that they had left on the ground where the action took place: therefore a flag of truce was immediately sent to the commander of the French army, to send a sufficient quantity of surgeons to attend to these wounded men, or else they should be left to the mercy of the Spaniards. And if that had been the case, it is most likely the poor unfortunate fellows would have had very middling treatment, for in that province the Spaniards were very inveterate against the French.

The enemy continued retreating, taking the nearest direction to Valladolid, (which was about twenty-four leagues from Salamanca), and our army continued advancing in like manner, forming our camp as convenient to wood and water as possible every night. But nothing in particular happened till we came to Valladolid, from which place a division of the enemy took a fresh route towards Madrid, and the main body formed a line about one league beyond Valladolid.

In consequence of this party taking a fresh route in a quite different direction, our army was obliged to halt; and our division, together with the light division and a regiment of cavalry, were immediately dispatched off in pursuit of them, leaving the remaining part of our army at camp, near Valladolid, to watch the manœuvres of the other part of the enemy

Having commenced our march towards Madrid, in pursuit of that party, we encamped every night, taking our route through Portillo, and by Segovia, and so on by and through many other towns and villages, till we came to Madrid, which was more than thirty leagues. Nothing in particular happened on this march. When

we came to Madrid, we found that this party of the
enemy had placed themselves in a large fort on one
side of that city.

Madrid is the capital of Spain, but I cannot give
any account of the place, for it was getting dark when
we entered the city, and we marched right through, with
drums beating and colours flying, without making any
halt whatever: therefore all that we could see was a
crowd of people: for the streets were so crowded, that
we could hardly pass. We were nearly two hours in
marching through, and when we came to the other side
of the city, where this fort was, we formed our camp
round it, so that the enemy should not make their escape, for their fortification was not altogether very
strong; in consequence of which, it was our intention
to make an attack as soon as possible. But however,
they did not give us that trouble, for on the following
morning, about nine o'clock, they surrendered themselves prisoners of war without a shot being fired. This
party consisted of about three thousand; so they were
delivered up to an escort of the Spaniards, and next
morning, soon after day-light, we commenced our march
back towards Valladolid, taking nearly the same route as
we came, and encamped every night as before.

When we arrived at Valladolid, we took up our
quarters in the town, for the enemy were still in the
same position, about one league distant, and had made
themselves small huts, ranged regular in line, by companies, as if they intended to remain there some time:
so by that, we were in hopes of having a few days' rest.

after so long a march. But however our rest did not continue long, for on the following morning, before break of day, the enemy began to retreat towards Burgos, and we immediately advanced in pursuit of them in the usual manner.

Nothing in particular happened till we arrived at Burgos, which was about twenty leagues from Valladolid: but there being a castle close to that town, in possession of the enemy, one division was left there, together with a party of engineers and a working party from our division, in order to lay siege to the castle, and the remaining part of our army advanced about three leagues further, and formed line about one league from the enemy; for they had taken up their position about four leagues beyond Burgos. So there we encamped in a regular way, but without tents; and about one hour before break of day, we stood to our arms in the usual manner, and continued under arms till it was quite broad day-light, and as soon as our general officers were fully satisfied that the enemy were making no movement, we were dismissed, and parties immediately sent out for wood and water for the purpose of cooking, while our butchers were killing and dressing our meat.

There we remained, as comfortable as the weather would permit us, till towards the latter end of October; but no engagement took place while we remained there, which was about six weeks. Several attacks were made to take the castle, but it being so strongly fortified, they proved unsuccessful. Burgos is a large town, but not fortified; the castle is close to the town, and stands on a hill, with very strong fortifications all round, and commands the town.

While we remained at this place, the enemy received a strong reinforcement of troops from France; and on the 22d of October, they began to advance with a much superior force, in consequence of which, we were obliged to retreat, for our army was then getting very weak by sickness, being obliged at that time of the year to encamp without tents.

The day previous to our retreat, the enemy's cavalry advanced to within one mile of our line, upon which we stood to our arms and began to advance in order to meet them: but as soon as they found us advancing, they retreated; but we continued advancing for nearly two miles, and then halted and sat down, but no skirmishing took place. So we remained on our ground till about seven o'clock in the evening, when we began to retreat, and continued on till four o'clock the next morning, when we halted and lay down about two hours; but finding the enemy advancing very rapidly, we stood to our arms again, and continued retreating all day till it was nearly dark, then we formed our camp, and remained till about four o'clock in the morning: we then stood to our arms in the usual way, and continued our retreat till nearly sun-set in the evening, when we arrived on the other side of Palencia, towards Valladolid: there our division formed our camp very convenient to the river Pisuera, at about four miles distance from Palencia, where was a bridge, near Villa

Murial. Our regiment was ordered to defend this bridge, and soon after dark at night, a party of engineers was set to work, boring the bridge, in order to blow it up.

We remained there very quiet till about nine o'clock on the following morning, the 25th of October, 1812, when we discovered a division of the enemy advancing at a very short distance from us, in consequence of which, about two hundred of our regiment were placed very convenient to the bridge, and the remaining part of the regiment was extended along the river.

The enemy seeing so small a party left to defend the bridge, they made a grand push for that place; but fortunately, before they could make their object, the bridge blew up, which put a stop to their pursuit: so then they extended themselves along the river, in about the same direction that we were, by which a sharp skirmishing immediately took place, and continued about four hours. One company of our regiment was very convenient to a grist-mill that was on this river, and while they were busily skirmishing with the infantry that was on the opposite side of the river, a troop of the French cavalry rushed out from behind the mill, quite unawares to us, and swept away the whole company as prisoners of war before we could give them any assistance. The remaining part of our brigade was formed along the river on our right, which continued skirmishing in about the same manner; but at length, having kept up a continual fire for nearly four hours, it was thought necessary for us to fall back a little, and place a brigade of Spaniards in our places for a while, in order for us to have a little rest: therefore being relieved, we fell back about half a mile to some rising ground, and sat ourselves down.

From that place we could plainly see with the naked eye the whole of the French army, which was formed on the plains; their numbers were so great, that the fields appeared to our view almost black. We had not been sitting more than half an hour, when we beheld the enemy fording the river, and the Spaniards retreating in an unsoldier-like manner; in consequence of which our brigade was again ordered to stand to our arms and give them a charge, which we immediately did with great vigour, and in a few minutes we captured about four hundred prisoners; there were also a great number killed and wounded in endeavouring to make their escape back across the river: therefore they did not make any further attack that day. The loss of our regiment on this occasion consisted of one lieutenant and about fifty men taken prisoners, and about seventy killed and wounded.

We remained on our ground that night, and on the following morning, about four o'clock, we stood to our arms and continued our retreat, and on the 27th, crossed this river Pisuera about five or six miles from Valladolid, and encamped about four miles to the left of that town. Next day, we crossed the river Douro at Trudella, from thence we took our route through Rueda; a few miles from that place we halted two days. From thence we took our route to Salamanca, there we halted several days. Nothing in particular happened with our division from Villa Murial to this place, which I consider to be more than thirty leagues; but at length the enemy began to approach us very rapidly, and not having a sufficient force to attack them, we were obliged to recommence our retreat towards Ciudad Rodrigo. The enemy pursued us so closely, that as we were leaving Salamanca on one side, the enemy were coming in on the other side; and some skirmishing took place every day. Our divison and one more, together with some cavalry, formed one column under the command of Lieutenant General Sir Edward Paget.

We made our retreat to Ciudad Rodrigo in the best manner that we could: the weather and the roads were then very bad, and in consequence of so much rain, the rivers began to run very strong, and every brook and ditch was overflowing with water; so that I might venture to say, that we had several brooks or rivers to ford more or less every day: In consequence of that, and for want of food and regular rest, our army began to straggle and get very much fatigued, so that many were left behind, who, we might easily suppose, fell into the hands of the enemy.

The distance from Salamanca to Ciudad Rodrigo is about twenty leagues: between those two cities our army sustained great loss. The third day's march from Salamanca, we were obliged to be very alert, for the enemy's cavalry being so close to our heels, and having a strong river to ford, several regiments were obliged

97

to form themselves into a solid square while the others were getting over. Our cavalry exerted themselves to their utmost, in order to check the enemy's advance; and at length we crossed the ford with not a very great loss, but skirmishing continued the greater part of the day; and notwithstanding all our exertions, by some means or other, Lieutenant General Sir Edward Paget was taken prisoner on that day. On the fore part of the follbwing day some sharp skirmishing took place; but as we began to approach Ciudad Rodrigo, or at least within a few miles, the enemy's advance began to shorten their pace, and in the evening they fell back a little, in order to join their main body; and next day, being the 19th of November, 1812, we encamped near Ciudad Rodrigo, and the French army retreated towards Salamanca.

In consequence of this, orders were given out for our army to fall back into Portugal, and take up their different cantonments for the winter season. Our division received orders to proceed to Lamego in Portugal, which was about eighteen or twenty leagues from Ciudad Rodrigo. Lamego is a large town, about one league from the river Douro, and about nine from Oporto, which town is close to the mouth of the Douro.

On this short march from Ciudad Rodrigo to Lamego, we took up our quarters in the different towns and villages every night, making regular stages, taking our direction through Celerico, which was formerly a fine town, but during the late war it had been very much damaged by the enemy. Some of the buildings

K

were burned down, and others left in a shattered ruin-
ous condition. But however, that was not the only
town that was so much damaged by the enemy; for most
of the towns in Portugal, that they had been in, were
left in about the same condition; for I have marched
through several places in pursuit of them, where not a
window shutter or door could hardly be seen, and as
for furniture, that was quite out of the question, for
that was the first thing they would destroy.

This part of Portugal is a rough, mountainous,
hilly country, and mostly covered with shrubs, bushes,
and ragged rocks; and in some places a great quantity
of very large stones lying on the surface of the ground;
in my opinion, some are as large as wind-ricks or small
wheat-ricks that are made in our country. There are
some vineyards it is true, and here and there an olive
orchard and a few chesnut trees; there are also some
hares and rabbits frequently to be seen. The streets in
the towns and villages are very narrow, and the roads
about the same, and in general so very bad, that we
frequently found great difficulty in getting our guns
along. It was also dangerous marching in the night,
for in some places we might tumble over loose stones
that lay in the road, almost as big as our knapsacks;
and in other places, tumble headlong into great holes.
But when on the march in the night, we formed a plan
among ourselves, to follow each other's track as near as
possible, so that if the man in front should stumble,
the next might be some little aware.

99

The roads in Spain are in general much better than they are in Portugal: but however, the ways of the inhabitants, in most of the villages in Portugal, very well agree with the manner of the country; for it is certain, they live in a very dirty beastly way. Their houses are built with stone, in a very rough miserable looking manner; and in such houses as have one floor above the ground, that is generally the place the family live in; and on the ground floor under where they live, is the stable or pigsty; perhaps one window with no glass, which is secured at night with a shutter. Some of their inside rooms are without any window whatever, and no other light but what comes in at the door when opened; their fires are placed on a stone close to the wall, sometimes in one corner of the room, with no chimney whatever; the smoke makes its way through the window or doorway, or otherwise through the roof; for the roof is not pointed, or as I might say, not plastered, to keep out either wind or weather.

Most of the houses, that belong to the lower class of people, are very mean, mostly only a ground floor, and perhaps no other light than what comes in at the door, or at least at a hole made in the upper part of of it; but certainly, they have some little light that comes in through the roof. In many of these poor habitations the fire is placed in the middle of the house; their seats are some rough-made stools or blocks of wood. Some of the natives, perhaps half naked, and as yellow with smoke and dirt as a parcel of tawnies, some covered with vermin, in this manner will huddle round a bit of fire, to all appearance as comfortable as they that live in a palace.

They have no pots or kettles for their cooking, they boil their victuals in earthen jars which they call penellas, which are something like small pickling jars in our country. I have often seen the poor people go out to the fields and gather some sort of herbs, which they cut small, as we do pot herbs, and put it into one of these penellas with some water, and place it on the hearth stone before the fire, and when it is nearly fit for use, they will put a table-spoonful of oil into it, or more, according to the quantity of vegetables, and with this and a piece of bread made from Indian corn, they will make a hearty meal.

So now having arrived at Lamego, we took up our winter quarters in the different villages round that town, where it was most convenient: our regiment occupied Villa Meom, one league from Lamego.—Here ends our campaign for this year.

While we remained at this place, we got good provisions, and very regular; also, some other articles that were needful, in particular shoes and shirts; for at that time we were got very bare of both these articles; and in a few days after we were supplied with every thing that was necessary, we received the balance of six months arrears of pay that were due to us; for during this campaign, we never received any money whatever. But however, that was not half so mortifying to us as being short of provisions; for if we lost three days' provisions out of four, (which we several times did), we never got a bit more than our allowance at any other time when it could be got, and we always paid the same if it was ever so short; so that there was not the least encouragement when we were short.

From the time that we left Travanca, in January, till we came to Lamego, in November, I consider that we had marched more than fourteen hundred miles; but however, having good provisions, rest, and a little money to purchase a few bottles of good wine, all past fatigues were soon smothered. So we remained in our cantonments very comfortable till May, and in the course of this time, several regiments joined the army from England or from some foreign stations; and most regiments in the army were joined by detachments from the depots in England, and small parties also frequently joined from the different hospitals; so that our army was daily increasing.

On the 6th of May, 1813, being well clothed and in good health, we began our advance in pursuit of the enemy once more. This was a bold advance, and which led to the total defeat of the French army, for they were never afterwards victorious.

The first day's march, we crossed the river Douro in some Portuguese boats, about five miles from Lamego, and marched to Villa Real, where we took up our quarters for that night; but from that town, we encamped every night, making regular stages for about a month, taking our directions by Mirandela, in Portugal, and so on into Spain, leaving Zamora a few miles on our right. But in consequence of the river Ezla

K 3

being so deep, we were detained two or three days waiting for a bridge to be made, for there was no possibility of the infantry crossing the ford. Some of our cavalry crossed, but as the current ran so strong, several were carried away and drowned.

As soon as the bridge was made, we crossed the river, and from thence took our direction through Tora, by Palencia, towards Burgos; but as we approached within a few miles of that place, the enemy evacuated the castle, and blew up some of the principal fortifications; therefore we passed by that town.

During this long advance, nothing in particular happened with our division till the 18th of June, when we fell in with a division of the French army near Frias, quite unawares to us, when on our regular line of march, about the middle of the day. The fourth division of our army was in pursuit of this party, but as the enemy took a different direction in the night, the lot fell on our division; therefore a sharp contest took place, which continued more than two hours; but at length the enemy began to retreat so rapidly, that our division was halted, and the light companies dispatched in pursuit of them. So we continued advancing, driving them before us like a flock of sheep for nearly two leagues, giving them a few shots when most convenient. They would also give us a few shots sometimes, but as we pursued them so closely, they had not much time to give us many; for only five of our company were wounded on this occasion; and night coming on, that put an end to our pursuit. So then we were ordered to

103

fall back to the division the same night. We should much rather have kept our ground, for we stood in need of a little rest, instead of marching two leagues back; nevertheless, as we were so small a party, it was necessary to fall back, so we joined the division about midnight.

On the following morning, soon after day-light, we advanced in pursuit of the enemy again, but we did not overtake them any more till the 21st of June, 1813, on which day the glorious and ever memorable battle of Vittoria was fought. The night previous to the battle, we formed our camp about two leagues from Vittoria, on a sort of wild wilderness place, among brambles, thorns, &c. and to my thinking, almost all sorts of vermin; but nevertheless, in the evening, after we had got our bit of meat and cooked it, which was not long about, for most of us broiled it on some fire coals, having nothing to eat with it, we laid ourselves down two or three in a place, where it was most convenient; but hearing such music with the vermin crawling and running about among the leaves, and sometimes running over us, caused our rest to be but middling that night.

About one hour before day-light, we stood to our arms in the usual manner, as we always did when convenient to the enemy, as before mentioned, and remained till broad day-light: during which time our commissary arrived with half a pound of bread for each man, but nothing else; but however, that with a drop of good water was very acceptable, for we had then been three days without bread. We were several times, on this long

advance, short of provision, the reason why is this:—
when the army was advancing in pursuit of the enemy,
we frequently marched double stages, in consequence of
which the cattle that carried our provisions were not
able to come up with the army according to the time
appointed; therefore by that means, we were obliged
to do without it till it did come, let the time be long
or short.

Now having got that half pound of bread, we advanced, about five o'clock in the morning, towards
Vittoria, knowing the enemy were there waiting to receive us. We had then about two leagues to go, as
before mentioned; and between nine and ten o'clock,
we arrived on a hill about one mile from Vittoria, where
we had a fine view of the greater part of the French
army; for they had formed all ready for combat along
the river for three or four miles each way. On one
side of Vittoria is a plain or a sort of marsh, on which
place they were like swarms of bees; for the whole of
their baggage, together with three waggon-loads of
money, (which they had got to pay the army), were
all formed up regular, in readiness to follow our army;
for they thought to drive us down the country again, in
about the same manner as they did from Burgos; or at
least, they told the inhabitants of Vittoria, that such was
their intention; and so it plainly appeared, for we hardly
ever knew them to exert themselves as they did at this
place; but notwithstanding all their exertions, they
could not accomplish their design.

105

In a few minutes after our arrival on the hill, our division received orders to proceed to Gamava, a village about three miles to the left of Vittoria, at which village the enemy were very numerous, with a large column placed at the bridge, and also a quantity of riflemen placed along the river. We advanced to the village in open column of companies; the light companies formed the advance, about one hundred yards in front; and when we came near, the first thing that the enemy saluted us with was a few cannon shot, for they had guns placed in all directions; but as soon as we got within gun-shot distance, we advanced to the village in double quick time, and gave them a grand charge, by which we got full possession of the village in a few minutes, and the light companies were immediately extended along, very convenient to the river, just opposite their skirmishing party, with an order not to expose ourselves more than we could help, nor to advance one inch without an order: therefore we formed ourselves under cover of a bit of a bank that was about knee high, and in this position we continued skirmishing for more than two hours—the remaining part of the division kept possession of the village.

The enemy made several bold attacks to force the bridge, in order to regain the village, but were repulsed every time with great loss; it was a very narrow street that led to the bridge, which was a great disadvantage to us, and their guns continued roaring tremendously; it was much in comparison to a continual thunder, for they never ceased throwing shot and shells into the village during the action, by which most of the houses were very much damaged.

It plainly appeared this day, that the enemy had formed a sort of determination not to be beat, for we never saw them stand so vigorous before; but notwithstanding all that, between four and five o'clock in the afternoon, we gave them another grand charge at the bridge, in consequence of which there was great slaughter on both sides, but in a few minutes the enemy gave way, upon which we pushed on more vigorous, and got full possession of the bridge; and all of a sudden the whole French army retreated, leaving one hundred and eighty pieces of cannon, about four hundred ammunition waggons, the whole of their baggage, provisions, and cattle, together with three waggon-loads of money, and many carriages that belonged to their generals and other officers of high rank, (several with their ladies and families in them); and among the crowd was Joseph Bonaparte's carriage and lady. The whole fell into our hands, and also many prisoners; but however, we did not stand worshipping that, for we pursued the enemy about one league as close as possible, by which more prisoners were taken; but before our guns could pass over the bridge, some men were obliged to move the dead bodies, for they lay in heaps most melancholy to behold. Notwithstanding, our regiment got off rather favourably in this engagement, for I believe not more than one hundred were killed and wounded, but some other regiments suffered very much.

107

So now having formed our camp, we fortunately beheld a field of beans very convenient to us, and just fit for use, and although we were rather fatigued, the field was swarming with soldiers in a few minutes, and before dark, there was hardly a bean to be found in the field. While some were gathering the beans, others were looking out for something to eat with them; for at this place we were not refused of getting something to eat if we could find any, although we never had been favoured with such liberty before; and as some of our regiment were searching about a village that was but little more than half a mile from our camp, they had the good fortune to find a great quantity of good flour, which they happily loaded themselves with, and brought it into the camp: so we all got as much flour as supplied our wants that night, and some to carry with us for another time. No bread could be found, but having plenty of flour and green beans with our meat, we all made a most noble supper: but still there was one thing that most of us were short of, that was salt to season our supper.

Now after we had filled our bellies, we sat and amused ourselves over what had passed during the day; in the mean time our commissary arrived with a pint of wine for each man, which occasioned our conversation to continue a little longer; and in the course of this evening I was promoted to the rank of a serjeant. So now night having approached, we laid ourselves down on the turf, under the branches of the trees, as comfortable as all the birds in the wood; for the enemy continued retreating nearly all the fore part of the night.

On the following morning, soon after day-light, we advanced in pursuit of the enemy in the usual manner: we continued advancing till about three o'clock in the afternoon, when our division was countermanded to proceed towards Pampeluna, in Spain; therefore we turned back the same road, about one league that night, to a town, the name I cannot remember, where we took up our quarters in a convent; but most of us would much rather have been in the fields as usual, for the enemy had left it in such a filthy miserable condition, that it could not be wholesome to be in; and what was still more remarkable, this was the first night's quarters that we had in any house or harbour since we left Villa Real, in Portugal, on the 6th of May; having marched since that period more than three hundred miles: but however, we were supplied with three days' good provisions in that town,—we were very seldom short of provisions after the battle of Vittoria.

Next morning we marched at day-light, and encamped in the evening near Vittoria; and from thence we took the direct road to Pampeluna, and continued our march till the third day, when we arrived in sight of that town, within about two leagues; but when on our regular line of march, about the middle of the day, our route was countermanded, to return immediately and proceed to St. Sebastian in Spain, with all speed. So we turned back the same road to Vittoria, and from thence between the Pyrenean Mountains, by Tolosa, and through Arnami to St. Sebastian, making long stages every day. There we formed our camp behind a hill, about one mile from the town.

St. Sebastian is a garrison town on the sea coast, about three leagues from France. It is surrounded by the sea, except one narrow neck of land that leads to it. There is a very strong fortified castle in the town, that stands on a very steep hill. There was also a convent about a quarter of a mile from the town, close to the road that led to it, in which place the enemy had secured themselves. This convent was the first thing that took our attention, for nothing could be done till we could get possession of that place; therefore a battery was formed, as quick as possible, within two hundred yards of the convent, and continued firing into it three days, by which time great part of it was beat down about their ears; but in spite of all that, they kept possession. Then orders were given for a party of the Portuguese brigade, that belonged to our division, to make an attack and storm that convent, and to be supported by the 9th regiment in case of necessity. Therefore, according to order, that brigade advanced towards the convent about ten o'clock in the forenoon, on the 17th of July, and our regiment very convenient in their rear. Our company and one more were in a different direction to the regiment, where the enemy had made a sort of redoubt, a little distance from the convent on the left. Between the enemy and us was a narrow lane, with a high growing hedge on each side; and as soon as the enemy found of our approaching, they placed themselves along the hedge on their own side, and the Portuguese in like manner placed themselves along this side of the lane, and commenced firing through both hedges: there they continued firing, in that way, for about a quarter of an hour, without making any sort of attempt any further. But at length, Lieutenant-Colonel Cameron, who commanded our regiment, got quite out of patience in waiting; upon which he ordered the regiment to advance by the Portuguese, and make an attack. Our officer could not see the regiment, neither had he any knowledge of its advancing; but fortunately, Lieutenant Ogle, who commanded our company that day, ordered us to advance and make an attack on the redoubt, just at the same time as the regiment attacked the convent; by which we got full possession of both places in a few minutes, driving the enemy before us into the town. The loss of our regiment, on this occasion, consisted of our colonel slightly wounded, one captain killed, two lieutenants wounded, and about sixty men killed and wounded.

Now having got full possession of the convent, the next thing was to make preparations for an attack on the town; therefore our engineers were set to work as soon as possible, making batteries and intrenchments, in order to make a breach to storm the town. One battery was formed where the enemy's redoubt was, which proved to be a very disagreeable job; for some part of our work happened to come across their burial ground, where many had lately been interred, so that we were obliged to remove them and bury them elsewhere. Some were then in a putrified state, without any thing wrapped round them, and some would fall to pieces while being removed. At this place many dead bodies were burned, but for what reason I cannot ascertain, unless it was for fear the smell would cause some bad distemper.

But however, having our battery completed, and a breach made, orders were given for an attack to be made to storm the town. Therefore, on the 25th of July, about eleven o'clock at night, we commenced the attack, but unfortunately without success; for the breach was small, and so steep, that we found great difficulty in getting up, and the enemy continued pouring down their small shot and hand-grenades from all quarters; but in spite of all, we forced our way in. But what was still more aggravating, when we had got possession of the breach, to our surprise the enemy had thrown a large fire across the passage that led into the town, so that there was no possibility of getting any further; therefore all that we could do then, was to get back as well as we could, which we did, but not without the loss of a great number of brave British soldiers, in particular the 1st Royal Regiment of foot, who were the greatest suffererers. Several gallant officers lost their lives in this unfortunate attack, among whom was Lieutenant-Colonel Crawford, who was second in command of the 9th regiment. After this, it was thought most proper to batter down the town walls by a heavy cannonading; therefore an express was immediately dispatched off, for the battering train to make all speed to

L 2

this place: so in about three days, the battering train arrived, and our work was put into execution as soon as possible.

About this time, a sharp engagement took place with the remaining part of our army on the Pyrenean Mountains, about four or five leagues from this place; in consequence of which, an order came for our division to hold themselves in readiness to leave this town at the shortest notice, unless further orders: therefore, our intrenching tools, &c. were immediately packed up, in readiness to march, and some of our heavy guns were put on board our shipping: but however, our army having got the upper hand of the enemy, the order was countermanded, and we were to remain and recontinue the siege. So our guns were disembarked again, and also some more heavy guns from on board the shipping, together with a sufficient number of sailors to man them.

As soon as our batteries were completed, a heavy cannonading commenced, which continued about three days, by which time a large breach was made. During this time, the enemy continued very busy, making preparations for our destruction, by forming a mine a little distance within the breach, in order to blow us up as soon as we entered. But the Almighty so ordered it, that they did not accomplish their design in that point; for fortunately, about three or four days before we made the attack, a French serjeant deserted from the town, and gave us information about that mine.

113

So now the breach being sufficiently wide, and such arrangements made that were needful, orders were givèn for the storm; and on the 31st of August, 1813, about ten o'clock in the morning, we began the grand attack; and having some knowledge of the mine that the enemy had prepared inside of the breach, we were some little aware: therefore three false attempts were made in order to banter the enemy to spring that mine. The two first attempts that we made were without effect; but the third, we made more vigorous, as if we were determined to enter, by which they sprung their mine; but fortunately, instead of catching us in that trap, they blew up a number of their own men; and immediately after the mine exploded, we made a grand push, and got full possession of the breach in a few minutes; and it was astonishing to see what a quantity of the enemy lay sprawling by the explosion of their mine. But we yet found something to do before we could get possession of the town; for the enemy had so blockaded the streets, that we found great difficulty in making our way through. They had formed a sort of breast-work, with barrels of sand, across the streets in several places, which was a great disadvantage to us; for when we had drove them from one place, there was another before us; and they continued pouring down small shot on us from all quarters. But however, in spite of all their exertions, in about one hour we got full possession of the town, driving the enemy to the castle, where they were obliged to fly for refuge.

114

By some means or other, in this attack some part of the town caught fire; in consequence of which a great part of it was burnt to ashes before it could be extinguished; and many houses had already been burnt during the siege, very probably by the explosion of our shells that were thrown in. Our loss in this attack was very great, both of officers and soldiers. But the castle did not command the town, for it being situated on so steep a hill, they could not bring one gun to bear on the town: therefore we could keep possession without much fear.

In the afternoon of this day, the enemy sent out a flag of truce, requiring the suspension of hostilities for fourteen days, unless they should be relieved, and if not, at the expiration of that time it was to be evacuated, and the whole of the troops and other effects in garrison should be marched to France with the honours of war. But Lieutenant-General Sir Thomas Graham, who commanded at this place, made an objection to that proposal without any hesitation. So then it was thought proper to place some guns on the horn-work, to play on the castle, (in addition to our former batteries) which was done without delay; and on the — of September, about ten o'clock in the morning, we commenced firing on the castle with more than forty pieces of cannon; in consequence of which, every gun that they could bring to bear on us was silenced in a very short time. There were also many shells thrown in, which caused great slaughter among them. This

115

continued about four hours, and then Sir Thomas Graham gave orders to cease firing, and sent in a flag of truce to know on what other conditions they would surrender: their answer was, they would surrender on such conditions as they had already proposed. So then we recommenced firing with every gun that could be used, and our thundering cannons roared tremendously for about half an hour more, when they surrendered themselves prisoners of war.

About two thousand were then in the garrison, including officers, sick, and wounded. Their loss was unknown to us: but our loss during the siege was very great; and in two or three days after the surrender, a statement of the killed and wounded was made, which amounted to more than two thousand of our division, besides officers.

Our division, which was called the fifth division, commanded by General Leith, consisted of two brigades of British infantry, and one brigade of Portuguese, besides some British artillery. The first brigade, commanded by General Hay, was the 1st Royals, the 9th, and 38th regiments; the second brigade, commanded by General Robinson, was the 4th, 30th, and 44th regiments; the Portuguese brigade was the 3d and 13th regiments, and the 8th Cacadores. Among the number of wounded, I was one of the unfortunate sufferers, having received a severe wound in my left arm.

So now the prisoners being secured, orders were given for the wounded to be conveyed to the different hospitals in the rear of the army, and a large party was

put on board two transport ships at Passages, between
France and St. Sebastian, in which party I was one.
There we remained three days, expecting orders to sail
for England; but it did not happen to be such good
luck, for instead of that, we received orders to put to
sea, and steer our course for Bilboa, in Spain. So on
the following morning, soon after day-light, we put to
sea with a fair wind and very pleasant weather: but
nevertheless, being on board a ship without beds or
hammocks, you may easily suppose it was very uncomfortable for wounded men; for sometimes when the
ship rolled with the swells of the sea, the cries and
groans of some were enough to make any person's
heart ache. Several died of their wounds, while on
board, whose bodies were committed to the sea.

However our voyage was but short, for on the
third day in the afternoon, we came to an anchor close
to our hospital, in the river Ybaicabal, which led to Bilboa. Bilboa is a large town about three leagues from
the sea; our hospital was about half way between the
sea and that town, and had been formerly built for the
purpose of a rope-walk, but to all appearance it had
not been much in use. It was two stories high, and
having a good boarded floor on the second story, it
made a middling good hospital. This was such an
hospital as is seldom to be seen, for there were about
thirteen hundred men in it, all wounded; and what is
most remarkable, about twelve hundred were in one
room, for there was no partition to divide us from one
end of the hospital to the other, which was of a great

117

length. There we lay for nearly two months without
any beds or bedding, excepting our blankets that we
always carried about with us, and I might venture to
say, that more than one-third were without that; for
such men as were severely wounded, and brought
to this hospital by land, had lost every individual thing
that belonged to them, except their clothing which they
had on, and most likely that had not been taken off
since they had been wounded; therefore you may easily
suppose what sort of a condition we were in. There
was one thing still worse, that was the want of a good
surgery; for our wounds were dressed several days
with brown paper and oil, in consequence of which,
many of the wounds got in a very bad state. Neither
were there any utensils for the use of the hospital
during this time, except a few kettles that were purchased for to boil our meat in, and a few buckets for
night use. But what was the reason of being short of
these articles so long, I cannot ascertain; it was reported, that contrary wind was the reason: but however,
when those articles arrived, we were made as comfortable as possible.

Now as my brother had been so fortunate as to escape all danger hitherto, I will proceed a little further
with the regiment. Therefore, as the prisoners and
wounded were all secured, and every other arrangement made that was necessary, our division received
orders to evacuate St. Sebastian and join the army; and
about the middle of September, we marched and joined
the army on the Pyrenees, at about two leagues distance

118

from the river Bidasoa. The enemy were then on the other side of the river, a little distance within the borders of their own country.

We remained at camp on the Pyrenees till the 7th of October, 1813, at which time we received orders, about two o'clock in the morning, to stand to our arms and proceed to the river Bidasoa, to a place about one league from Fontarabia. The tide came up this river, so that there was no possibility of fording at all times; but when the tide was out, there was but little water. Nevertheless, we found great difficulty in crossing, for in some places the mud was nearly two feet deep. About one mile and a half distance from the river, on the other side, the enemy had formed a four-gun battery, which place our regiment was ordered to attack. Therefore, soon after break of day, on the 7th of October, as before mentioned, the tide being out, we crossed the river without any opposition. But we had not advanced more than one mile, before the enemy opened their battery on us, and their shots began to fly very sharp: nevertheless, we continued advancing very regularly in column of companies, till we got within musket-shot distance, and then we fired one volley and gave them a charge (according to English fashion) with as much vigour as the strength of our bodies would permit, by which we drove them from their battery and occupied their ground in less than fifteen minutes; and from thence we continued advancing and driving them before us for nearly two miles, when we were ordered to halt and cease firing, for we were getting very near

119

to their main body. I believe this was the first skir-
mish that took place in France; and to the best of my
knowledge, no other regiment besides the 9th was
engaged that day. So in the afternoon we took up our
position on some hills within about one mile of the
enemy's line.

Some time previous to this, the main body of the
enemy took up their position on a line of hills, and cut
down a large quantity of trees, which they placed along
the hills with the tops towards us, and the branches
made as picked as possible, in order to prevent our
army from advancing any further into their country.
Here our out-lying sentinels were posted within about
half a musket shot distance from the enemy's sentinels,
almost near enough to talk to each other; but they had
particular orders not to fire a shot, unless the enemy
should advance—neither did their centinels fire at us.

We remained at camp on the hills till the beginning of November; but at length Lord Wellington
seemed rather inclined to advance a little further into
the country, if by any means he could turn the enemy
from their position. So as there was no possibility of
forcing them, without the loss of an immense number
of men, it was thought most proper for a strong division of our army to advance round their left flank,
supposing that might be the means of moving them;
therefore on the 6th of November, very early in the morning, Lieutenant-General Sir Rowland Hill advanced
with his division in order to get round their flank, according to the proposal. Before break of day, we stood to

our arms in the usual manner; and soon after day-light, when the enemy found that our army was endeavouring to flank them, their whole line retreated all of a sudden, and we immediately advanced in pursuit of them with all possible speed, by which some part of our army was engaged very sharply in a short time.

But however, as it happened, it did not fall to our lot to partake of the engagement this time; so we advanced about two leagues that day towards St. Jean-de-Luz, and encamped where we halted; and as soon as night began to approach, we sat ourselves down, but were not permitted even to put our arms out of our hands during the night, for fear the enemy should make a sudden attack. But however, nothing in particular happened. On the following morning, soon after day-light, we advanced again; but the enemy retreated so rapidly through St. Jean-de-Luz, that not a shot was fired.

Close to that town was a large river, with a wooden bridge thrown over it that led into it; but what was rather mortifying to us, before we could reach that place, the enemy set fire to the bridge, so that we were obliged to ford the river, which ran very strong and was in some places nearly three feet deep. In consequence of this, some of our gun-carriages were placed in line across the river as close together as possible, so that if any men should be taken off their legs by the force of the water, it might be the means of saving their lives. Therefore, as the enemy continued retreating, we crossed the ford without the loss of a man, and advanced about one league further, but no engagement took place that day; for about noon, we took up our position at about two miles distance from the enemy, and in the course of the afternoon, we received orders to take up our quarters in the villages and straggling houses that were most convenient to the alarm post. Therefore, about sun-set, when our picquets were posted, and such arrangements made as were necessary, we went to our different stations, being about three leagues from Bayonne. A general order was immediately given out, That if any man should ill-use, plunder, or defraud any of the inhabitants, in any respect whatever, he should suffer death, or such other punishment as by a general court-martial should be awarded.

So now being in quarters, and having such orders, we supposed, or at least we were in hopes, that fighting and other hard fatigue was over for that season, for the enemy had taken up their quarters as well as we. But however, it was not long before we found ourselves rather mistaken; for on the 9th, 10th, and 11th of December, 1813, we had to try our skill again three successive days: I shall therefore detail them as follows:

The 9th, we stood to our arms about four o'clock in the morning, and began to advance, and soon after day-light, our advanced guard commenced skirmishing with the enemy's picquets; in consequence of which, it was not long before our division fell in with the main body, but whether our whole army was engaged or not I cannot ascertain, for our division was on the left flank of our army. So we continued skirmishing and advancing till we drove them within two miles of Bayonne; but in consequence of their having several batteries made, and also some guns placed on the main road that led to Bayonne, it was thought necessary to halt, which we did, but skirmishing continued till nearly sunset. About seven o'clock in the evening, we received orders to fall back to our former position again, and our regiment formed the rear guard on the main road, in order to cover the retreat of our wounded. So we formed close column, and retreated in that manner all the way, which was about eight miles. The reason why we retreated in close column, was in order to be ready to form against cavalry at the shortest notice, supposing they should advance and attack us on the road; but however, that did not happen to be the case, and it was very fortunate, on our sides, that they did not; for in consequence of so much rain that had fallen, the road was very bad, and so deep in some places, that our hospital waggons could hardly be got along, and we were sometimes nearly half-way up our legs in a slough of dirt; and it being so very dark, we were all in a miserable pickle, as it was past midnight before we could reach our quarters.

On the following morning, being the 10th, we assembled in the usual way, and soon after day-light, we discovered the enemy advancing upon us in all directions, and in a short time our picquets were driven off their posts; in consequence of which we were ordered to advance (which we immediately did) to a

123

place that was pointed out to us by our commander, and between eight and nine o'clock a sharp engagement took place. The second brigade and the Portuguese brigade of our division were the first called up that morning, and our brigade formed a little distance in the rear as a reserve; and in this form we remained till towards the middle of the day, when it was thought necessary for us to advance and relieve the second brigade, for they had suffered very much; but the Portuguese brigade had not been engaged long, neither had they sustained but very little loss: therefore we advanced according to order, and relieved the second brigade, and they fell back to our ground in order to get a little rest; and as soon as we took up our position, we commenced an independent firing.

The Portuguese were a little distance on the left of our regiment, and a sort of a thicket of bushes and trees was between us; and soon after we relieved the second brigade, the enemy seemed to place their attention rather more on the Portuguese brigade than they had hitherto; nevertheless they fought as well as any soldiers need to do as long as the enemy kept at a distance, but as soon as the enemy made a bit of a charge, (which they did in about half an hour after we came up), the Portuguese immediately gave way, in consequence of which, our regiment was totally surrounded in a short time, and shots flew both front and rear. It being woody nearly all round us, we had but little knowledge what was going on only with the column that we were engaged with, and as the Portuguese

M 2

fell back so sudden, our general officers had no time to give us any information, neither did we form any idea of their retreating; but however, as soon as we found ourselves surrounded, we did not stand hesitating and considering what was best to do, but by an order from Gol. Cameron, who was still in command of our regiment, we immediately turned to the right about, and charged them man to man, by which we carried about four hundred prisoners on the point of the bayonet. We immediately delivered them up to the second brigade, which was just getting under arms to come to our assistance; but being so fortunate as to effect our escape without any help, we turned about again to our former object, for we could plainly see that a minute's delay might cause great confusion, for the enemy had advanced and almost got possession of our ground, upon which we gave them another charge; but the enemy seing us advancing so rapidly, they fell back a little, and we re-formed on our old position, and a sharp skirmishing still continued. They made several attempts to charge our line, but finding our shots fly so briskly, and we not willing to leave our ground, their hearts failed them before they came to the point of the bayonet, and so turned back again. This manœuvring and skirmishing continued till nearly sun-set, when they began to retreat, but we kept our ground, which put an end to that day's fatigue.

It was very woody where the French made this attack; but not much credit could be allowed to their valour. They thought to frighten us by their bold attempts, which might have been done, if there had been a possibility of depriving us of that renowned British courage which had so eminently distinguished us on every occasion.

So now night having approached us, and our picquets being posted, we lodged our arms and set to work making some fires, for at that time it was very cold; having done that, we placed ourselves round them and eat what little food we had got, and made ourselves as comfortable as our situation would allow, and in this manner we huddled round our fires and passed the greater part of the night; for we were not permitted to take off our accoutrements, neither to unfold our blankets during the night.

The next morning, being the 11th, soon after daylight, our regiment was ordered to advance up a little hill that was some distance in front; and according to order, we immediately advanced and formed upon that hill, and in a few minutes after, Lord Wellington and his staff ascended the hill in order to ascertain, if there was a possibility, whether the enemy were making any movement, and also what position they were in on this part of the line. But there was but one column that could be discovered at that moment, in consequence of which our light company was sent forward, and in a short time we were surprised by a skirmishing party of the enemy that was laid in ambush, and the shots began to fly very thick. Another company then advanced, and so on till five were sent out, by which we soon drove their skirmishers back. So now, after a little pause, the remaining part of our regiment was ordered to advance, which they did, and unfortunately, in a very short time we were obliged to fall back with the loss of one hundred and twenty or thirty men; for the enemy had several close columns formed in secret places, unknown to our commander, which caused us to sustain this loss. So now the division was ordered to advance: but I cannot give any further account of the engagement this day, for unfortunately in this attack my brother received a severe wound in his right arm, and was immediately sent to the rear, as that was a customary way on all such occasions as those, for fear the army should be obliged to retreat. Therefore as we are both wounded, I must leave the regiment at this place, within three leagues of Bayonne. My brother was put into hospital at Fontarabia in Spain, a town very convenient to the mouth of the river Bidassoa.

So now my campaign was finally ended, except about sixty or seventy miles that I had to march from Bilboa to Passages in Spain, at which place I embarked for England. But before I proceed to England, I will just step across to Bilboa, for in consequence of my arm being so severely fractured, I was obliged to remain there till towards the latter end of March, 1814; and while I was in that hospital, twelve pieces of bone were taken out of my arm, (and one piece was taken out when I was in the river Thames, on my passage to London); but at length my arm being in a fair way of getting well, and serjeants being wanted, I and one serjeant of the 61st regiment, who was also disabled, were sent off to Passages in charge of one hundred other disabled men, that were invalided, for England. So being provided with cars for the conveyance of our little baggage and such men as were lame, we commenced our march, taking our route through Zornoza, by Tolosa, through Arnami, to Rantera near Passages; there we were put into a chapel, and remained till the shipping were ready to receive us that were homeward bound. Our accommodation at this place was very middling, for the place was so crowded with stores and detachments that were going to the army, and such a number of wounded invalids bound for England, that we could scarcely find room to lie down; neither had we any convenience for cooking our provisions.

This was the place appointed for the embarkation of all that were homeward bound, and also for all stores, detachments, &c. going to the army, as this was the most convenient port near this part of the country. Here I made every enquiry about my brother, in order to know how he was or what had become of him; but I could get no intelligence whatever, by which I concluded that hé must either be dead, or gone to England.

So now a transport ship being ready, I embarked at Passages in company with about four hundred disabled men, and early in the morning of the 10th of April, 1814, being Easter Sunday, we put to sea with a fair wind, in company with two other transport ships, and also a man-of-war brig, which was our convoy. The wind blew rather hard, owing to which we found some difficulty in getting out of the harbour; for the mouth of that harbour is very narrow, with some high ragged rocks on both sides; but however, about the middle of the day, our little fleet was safe out, when a signal was made to make sail. When night began to approach, the wind still blowing very hard, our commodore came alongside as near as possible, and hailed the captain of our ship, giving him orders, " That if we " should be separated in the night by rough weather, " that Portsmouth was our intended destination; but " in case of necessity, we might put into the first " port that we could make." So we made all speed that was possible, and continued in company with the other ships till the fourth night, when the wind began to blow a heavy gale and the sea run very high, and it being so very dark, our situation was very alarming. The gale continued till near sun-rising next morning, when the wind began to abate, and fortunately we received no damage; but what became of our convoy and one of the transport ships, I know not, for we could see but one; neither did we see or hear any thing of them any more. So we continued to make all speed that was possible, and on the 17th we hove in sight of Plymouth, and in consequence of having some very bad cases on board, it was thought necessary to put into that port. Therefore towards the evening, we came to an anchor in Cawsand Bay, near Plymouth.

We had a surgeon on board it is true; or otherwise some unfeeling fellow, that was put in place of a surgeon; but certainly he could have no feeling for a poor wounded soldier; for he never examined our wounds but once during our voyage, until this day; in consequence of which some of the men's wounds began to fester and be in a very bad state. So now having come to an anchor, as soon as a boat could be got ready this unfeeling fellow went on shore, and reported what sort of a condition we were in, and that he thought us unfit to proceed any further by sea. Therefore on the following morning a signal was made for the ship to put into the harbour, which was done as soon as possible, and in the afternoon, being the 18th of April, 1814, we disembarked and those that had such bad wounds were ordered to be immediately taken to the military hospital.

As I was in good health, and my wound nearly well, I was appointed to see these orders executed; and when I came to the hospital, to my great surprise, almost the first man that I saw was my brother, who had arrived at this port a few days before; and in consequence of rough weather when on his passage home, he unfortunately fell down on the deck, and so injured his wounded arm, that it was expected for several days he must lose it.

So now the men's wounds having been examined by the head surgeons of the military hospital, a court of inquiry was immediately ordered for the examination of the surgeon that came home with us; and in a short time after, it was reported among us, that he was dismissed from his Majesty's service. Such men whose wounds were well or nearly so, were put into barracks at Plymouth Dock, where we were made as comfortable as we could wish, and the inhabitants showed us every mark of friendship. We remained there till about the middle of June, when orders were given for all such men as were not fit for any further service in the army, to be sent to Chelsea hospital, in order to pass the board.

Now by this time, my brother's wound was in a fair way of getting well, therefore we both embarked for London on board a transport brig, in company with about two hundred other disabled soldiers. We remained in the harbour two days, and in consequence of contrary winds, we were three weeks on our passage. At length we arrived in the river Thames, and came to an anchor close to Deptford, and on the following day we were taken up the river in some boats, and passed under London bridge, Black Friars, and Westminster bridge, and disembarked close to Chelsea college. We were put into quarters in Chelsea that night, but the place being so crowded with invalids, our party was ordered to be sent out to the villages. Therefore on the following morning we were sent to Putney, a village about four miles from Chelsea, in the county of Surrey, where we had very comfortable quarters, and as good accommodation as any soldiers could wish. In that village we remained till all our demands were settled to our satisfaction, in respect to back-pay that was due to us, and also two years' clothing that I had not received during my servitude in the 9th regiment. So now this being done, and every other arrangement made that was necessary, we were ordered to attend the board of Chelsea college, and on the 23d of August, 1814, I was admitted an out-pensioner of Chelsea hos-

131

pital at the rate of nine-pence per day, and my brother at one shilling per day.

On the 25th following, after providing ourselves with clothing and such articles as we stood most in need of, we commenced our march for Cirencester, taking our route the first day to Brentford; the 26th, to Nettlebed; the 27th, to Lechlade. This was the first night that we had been in our own county for several years; and to conclude my travels, it is rather remarkable, that the best quarters we could get in that town, was in a stable among a haggling team of horses. The 28th of August, 1814, we arrived at Cirencester, and there we still remain.

FINIS.

www.ingramcontent.com/pod-product-compliance
Lightning Source LLC
Chambersburg PA
CBHW022014160426
43197CB00007B/423